Autobiographies
of **Our Orgasms**

A Collection of Your Stories

Edited by Betsy Blankenbaker

CONTENTS

DEDICATION

For each person who wrote to me after reading
Autobiography of an Orgasm but is still too afraid to speak
up – these stories are for you.

INTRODUCTION

"Sex lies at the root of life and we can never learn to reverence life until we know how to understand sex."

—Havelock Ellis

"We've been taught that silence would save us, but it won't.

—Audre Lorde

I quietly released my first book, *Autobiography of an Orgasm*, **in November of 2014.** I self-published with no budget for media or PR. I decided to do the book release party in Miami, a place that had been home for the past seventeen years. The first venue I approached to host the book event turned me down. They didn't think the book aligned with their corporate image, which was ironic, because their website oozes sex appeal. The rejection was a first glimpse of the coming resistance to me speaking out about my body and sex. My friend Tara suggested I simply have the book event on the beach, and she offered to fly in from NYC to help me carry the books to the beach in a straw basket she had purchased in France. And so, over a hundred women with the combined superpower of about a million nerve endings among us, all committed to producing ecstatic states in our bodies, gathered at sunset to honor the release of a book about my five years of researching orgasm. That felt about right for a book that was about remembering our bodies as sacred and wired for pleasure.

Autobiography of an Orgasm was filled with a lifetime of secrets and shame about my body and my sensuality. I had only recently shared some

1

of the stories from the book with my mother, who is in her early eighties. She didn't say much or ask many questions, but once the reviews started coming in, she told me that she was proud of me for writing a book that was helping others.

When my friend, novelist Dan Wakefield, wrote an article about my book for *NUVO*, the alternative newspaper in my hometown in Indiana, he was cornered at a dinner party soon after by a woman who said, "Betsy's mother must feel awful about her writing the book."

Does that mean I should have stayed silent for my mother? Or for other women who may be uncomfortable about me speaking the truth about the female sexual experience? Or for ex-lovers? Would it affect future employment? What about my daughter and three sons? Did I owe it to them to stay silent – because who really wants their mom to write a book about orgasm?

Ultimately, I felt I couldn't afford not to speak up. Dr. Liz Orchard said, "Revealing the truths of our bodies creates a necessary path to breaking the cycle of silence and awakening the life force and powerful healer that resides in each of us - our orgasm."

Research shows that more than one in five women are unhappy with their sex lives. The medical industry diagnoses us with female sexual dysfunction. One common "solution" is to prescribe an anti-depressant. (It's a nearly three billion dollar solution). In her book, *Vagina*, Naomi Wolf writes, "…between one woman in five and one woman in three seems to be suffering from something very like sexual, or even like vaginal, depression."

Yet, in *Goddesses Never Age*, Dr. Christiane Northrup reminds us that "…women are wired to experience multiple orgasms because that moment of ecstasy is an expression of the life force accompanied by a burst of nitric oxide. Our bodies are not designed to limit or contain our pleasure. They are meant to experience it as the medicine it truly is."

In my study of BodyTalk energy medicine, I learned that orgasm and climax with a trusted, loving partner brings about ultimate state of health for both people. Why then are so many of us walking around with "depressed vaginas"?

I suspect the answer is multi-faceted. We don't understand how our bodies work. It is not difficult for a woman to orgasm when you understand that your orgasm starts with the first sensation you feel when your body is turned on. There are eight thousand nerve endings in a women's clitoris, solely dedicated to making her feel good. We were born with them, a gift from the Creator. Those nerve endings never go away, but if ignored, the pathways of energy that send doses of a feel-good hormone straight to our brains can't do their jobs, so we end up self-medicating with Prozac or alcohol, or we believe that it's hard for us to feel our orgasm and climax. It is not! Also, our culture rarely gives girls and women the message to honor their bodies as sacred. We wouldn't give ourselves away if we treated ourselves with reverence. Finally, in many cases, (I was one of them), our bodies may hold onto the shame or wounds resulting from sexual abuse. More than one in five women and one in twelve men have experienced some form of sexual assault on their bodies, many times it occurs during childhood. When too many of us stay quiet, we give our power away. When we don't speak up, we choose fear over love of our bodies.

I spent five years researching orgasm as a way to understand my body and its ability to feel ecstasy after a lifetime of feeling nothing. It's those inside wounds that we can't put band-aids on, so they stay with us for years until we either die with them, or we finally sit with them, like I did, when I wondered at the age of forty-five why I had a life that looked good but didn't feel good. With research and practice, I was surprised how quickly my body came back to life after I started to liberate my orgasm. (And you can do it, too.) I committed to training my body in the same way that Michael Jordan practiced basketball or Einstein committed to science, and I found that feeling orgasm and climax is as natural as experiencing the coolness of the breeze on my skin when I'm going for a walk.

In his book, *Science of Orgasm*, Barry Komisaruk writes, "I can well imagine how it would resonate with women who have cut themselves off from sexuality following abuse, but it strikes me that it can hit some powerful chords with women who have simply absorbed a lot of misinformation about orgasm over the years, too."

As I was writing *Autobiography of an Orgasm*, my daughter Lucy (who was twenty-three at the time and about to enter grad school) asked me if the book included anything about the importance of the brain. I was flustered by her question because I had spent years 'thinking and learning', and none of it made a difference to my orgasm or to my relationship to my body. I wanted Lucy to understand that the book was about what Rochelle Schieck, the creator of Qoya, wants us to do by "thinking less and feeling more" as a way to connect to our inner wisdom. I thought my story had nothing to do with my brain and felt like maybe I was disappointing my scholarly daughter by not pursuing a more academic path to fuel my brain. As I continued my research for this book, I found out orgasm absolutely is connected to the brain. Dr. Komisaruk reminds us that orgasm increases activity throughout the brain by flooding the brain with blood flow and oxygen. Orgasm is good for brain health as well as circulation, heart, lung, spinal cord and nerves. When you have a turned-on body, you are getting a great physiological and neurological workout. I suspect that our culture's overuse of pharmaceuticals and over-diagnosis of depression, sexual dysfunction and even ADD in adults would be radically affected if we each remember to honor our body as sacred and keep the neuro-pathways from our genitals and pelvic regions turned on so that our brains and our bodies can function in an ultimate state of health. We were born with these natural links within our bodies – why are we ignoring them?

My mother, Virginia Blankenbaker, was a former state legislator who truly dedicated her political life to serving people, especially women, children and the elderly. I watched my mother stand for issues when it wasn't socially, culturally or politically correct to do so. She was, and still is, a role model for me as a woman and a leader.

I came through the womb of my mother to be birthed into this world and I like the idea that my mom would want to give birth to a baby – who became a girl and then a woman – who spoke her truth rather than stayed quiet, even if it made her feel a little uncomfortable.

The women of the 1960s and 70s experienced social, political and economic freedom during the Women's Liberation movement, when women demanded equal rights, and men made more space for them to live fully as women. Why then with all this advancement (although women still make about 77 cents to the dollar for a man) and opportunity, are we still accepting that one in five of us has sexual dysfunction?

In *Vagina*, Wolf writes, "Female sexual pleasure, rightly understood, is not just about sexuality or just about pleasure. It serves, also, as a medium of female self-knowledge and hopefulness; female creativity and courage; female focus and initiative; female bliss and transcendence; and as a medium of sensibility that feels very much like freedom. To understand the vagina properly is to realize that it is not only coextensive with the female brain, but it is also, essentially, part of the female soul."

For fifty years, women have been liberated socially, politically and economically, but now is the time for the spirit of women to be liberated, and it will only happen if we take responsibility for liberating ourselves through listening to the wisdom of our bodies. This not only connects us to a life of feeling good, but also to a life of feeling God (or Divine Source, or choose your own word for Spirit).

This book is a collection of stories from women and men liberating their spirits and speaking the truth about their sensual experiences. A few of the writers chose to publish under pseudonyms because of concerns about judgment from family or former partners, or how it might affect their careers. All the writers are gutsy storytellers, and as I read each story, I connected back to a part of myself and felt a little more proud and powerful to show up fully, rather than to hide behind the parts of my life that at one time felt unacceptable or unspeakable.

After I released *Autobiography of an Orgasm*, my daughter Lucy sent me an excerpt from the book *Men Explain Things to Me* by Rebecca Solnit. Lucy had highlighted the following passage: "Some women get erased a little at a time, some all at once. The ability to tell your own story, in words or images, is already a victory, already a revolt."

Thank you to the soulful storytellers in this book for not staying quiet, for not letting yourselves disappear. Through your words you show us the tremendous ability of the human spirit to alchemize pain and disillusionment into realization of our bodies as holy. Reading your words inspires us and shows us how to liberate our spirits through connecting to the wisdom of our bodies.

—Betsy Blankenbaker

NOTE TO READERS:

This work is memoir. It reflects each writer's present recollection of his or her life. In some stories, certain names, locations, and identifying characteristics have been changed. Dialogue and events have been recreated from memory to convey the substance of what happened, and they represent each writer's recollection of the events.

ONE

The bend in the road is not the end of the road unless you refuse to take the turn.

—Anonymous

Dedicated to my aunt, Beth Hoover.
Birds of a feather soar together…

And with endless love to my daughter, Emma Rose,
whose heart remained tenaciously wide open when it
might have closed. You will make the very best doctor,
of course – one who is brave, brilliant, and deeply
caring.

THAT WOMAN'S VOICE
by Jeanne Louise Mayhue

I ran into a friend one day who had just posted on Facebook a beautiful photo of herself with her husband. They were outdoors and smiling, glowing together. I loved the picture, and I'd commented on the post, saying that they looked gorgeous. When I later saw her in passing, she said that she had thought of me while trying to decide whether or not to post it. She told me that I seem really comfortable sharing photos of myself and that she struggles with feeling confident in the same way. Without even giving myself time to process or consider the meaning of this moment for either of us, I kicked into gear, full-throttle humble, and the self-deprecating exchanges began. "Lately I feel like even my earlobes look older," I said. "My hair looks thin and awful a lot of the time," I assured us. Our time together was limited, but nevertheless we exchanged a satisfactory back-and-forth of mutual self-loathing and put-downs, while offering the other loving and reassuring compliments, and then we parted ways.

I realized later that day, while turning all this over in my mind, how fresh the conversation had felt, how ready I'd been with my stock responses. Why? Oh, right – because earlier in the week I'd already given the same performance. I'd stood in a salon with another lovely friend, and while looking at nail polish colors together, I showed her how ugly and huge my knuckles seem to me. "It's from having an autoimmune disease," I said. We talked about how I never, ever wear nail color on my hands, only my feet. "Because I don't like to highlight the knuckliness," I told her. "And look how curvy and weird my nail beds are," I offered after she had complimented my hands, describing her own as farmer's hands, and never pretty, holding them out for both of us to recognize the truth.

Check. Mate. We'd made sure to lower ourselves to a non-threatening and non-celebrated place where relationships are safe, or maybe we'd just shared vulnerable feelings in an effort to create intimacy. Maybe both. What I didn't say was, "Sometimes I feel knuckly, and sometimes I feel beautiful, but I'm leery of looking too seductive. I fear that women will turn on me, because I've experienced that before, and it's painful. I don't paint my fingernails. And I don't easily accept compliments – not without neutralizing the moment by declaring my flaws. I'm afraid that if I'm too confident, I'll invite the bull's-eye some woman will paint on my back, saying, as her brush creates smaller and smaller rings, "She thinks she's all that." And… boom. There it is.

It's my intention to live more authentically as I move forward in life, so while driving to school to pick up my children, I considered that cautious routine we move through together, we women, and my own familiar go-to phrases showed up: what I think five pregnancies have done to my thighs, or how I sometimes offer to reveal my stretch marks when someone says, "What!? I don't believe you even have five children!" We afford one another a graciousness, a kindness and an esteem which we don't always spare for ourselves. I thought of friends, my beautiful friends, and their unloving words about themselves. I've heard countless statements of defeat throughout the years. "Ugh, my war-torn ass, I'm so over it. I used to dance in the rain naked. I loved my body. I wouldn't do that now if my life depended on it!" or "I love those shoes, and I'd buy them – but my calves. They're so big. I just can't pull it off." Muffin tops, sagging eyes, thinning lips, inadequate breasts… I've heard it all, haven't you?

And so that day I was a little bit brave, just like my friend had been with her photo. I shared from my portfolio, posting pictures of myself in a swimsuit and rain boots, with text about how it felt to do that. The lighting was lovely, shadowy in black and white, with sunshine illuminating one side of the subject, me. I chose two photos, one a view of my body from the front, and the other a shot of the back side of me.

After sharing them, I thought I'd hear a few niggling inner whispers reminding me of reality. "Junk in the trunk" they'd surely say, in whose voice I can only speculate, perhaps in the chortling tone of an old joke originating somewhere in my family, one that had been retold many times and then, finally, mercifully, died away. You wouldn't think it now if your eyes took in all one hundred nine pounds of me, but I was a fairly robust toddler – my favorite kind! One day when I was two years old, I was lying on my back in someone's bed and had placed my naked, chubby toes on the newly painted bedroom wall, or so the story went. "Get your feet off the wall, you fat clod!" The words rang out, and were echoed in chorus for years after that day, followed by peals of laughter. It must have been my mother who put an end to it.

Far more likely, I suspected I would hear the voices of people I don't even really know: Students standing near their lockers, lining the halls of our high school, murmuring comments about the curvier, larger girls walking to class with their math and English books braced tightly across their chests, the same girls who had acquired their precious, unique curves earlier than most of us stick-straight daydreamers and were therefore considered by many to be sexually active. It had something to do with assuming that if you had the equipment, you were surely using it.

Surprisingly, none of those memories were what I processed. Those places were not what I visited after I hit "share" and the photos and written post were on my timeline, in everyone's newsfeed. Perhaps, because of what felt like an outpouring of gratitude and support in comments and in messages afterward, sentiments about identifying and words of love, my thoughts shifted to spiritual work, my truer deepening perspective, the one at play in this chapter of my life. I'd brought myself to stand in that place where the view, a vista really, is as quiet and holy as church. It's a place we carry with us always. Moreover it is who we *are*, but we often pretend instead that it is a destiny, and an elusive one reached by few.

And there I thought about other things that had been said, to me, as an adult. Words spoken by my ex-husband and father of my children, too humiliating and painful for me to share with others at the time, statements that more closely revealed my need for those photos. "Your breasts are ruined for me," he'd declared after the birth of our fourth child, standing there with his hands on his hips as I nursed in my nightgown and slippers, gently rocking my baby. And while pregnant with our fifth, I'd heard this observation, "We'll be able to hide homeless people in your vagina, or park a car in there. Jesus. That's what'll be left of your body."

These and numerous other perspectives he shared regularly, nonchalantly, politely even, as if he'd followed the statement with "And I like that dress on you. What's for dinner?" But the information he most frequently reminded me of, casually mentioning it without ever taking his eyes from the gaming screen he hunched over in seemingly permanent worship or from the road upon which he often raged, spilling our drinks while crayons flew and heads banged into windows, was this: "You know, if you ever leave me, I will kill you."

"Yes, I know," I'd reply.

As Facebook notifications grew in number, I closed my laptop and turned away. I remembered stepping over him in the morning where he lay passed out in his scotch-infused vomit, grateful that I hadn't woken up in bed covered in it and needing to wash my hair at 3am, again, tired from having sat up late next to him on the cold tile and wondering, while I watched to see that his chest still rose and fell, where I'd first send the children if I ever needed to bring medics or the coroner to our home. I had options. They were the same homes where later, during our legal separation, I'd sometimes hide my little ones when I sensed danger. Leaving them safe with friends, I would drive to a Starbucks in another area of town, swipe the debit card whose activity he constantly monitored online — a separate computer screen always open for tracking my whereabouts — and lead him elsewhere in pursuit of me until his rage subsided. Oftentimes people don't realize what lengths women will go to in order to avoid police arrest of their children's provider. A criminal record jeopardizes future employment, and no employment means no money for food or housing.

And of course, as I sat with him, contemplating options in my list of available neighbors who might discreetly help – mostly physicians with various on-call schedules, and trying not to fall asleep, I'd process the guilt I felt. Guilt because I was actually always a little relieved when he was several drinks on his way to this sad place. He was a very kind drunk, becoming softer and easier, smiling gently, freed of his own fury and disparaging humor for a while, and freeing us as well. He seemed "off the clock," in a "thank God it's Friday" kind of way. At all other times he was a full-time and severe sufferer of narcissistic and borderline personality disorders. I cried the day his diagnosis was not bipolar. I'd read plenty. A lifetime of that would have been far more manageable, medicable, and preferable than sharing this cage, I thought, albeit a gilded one.

But at least an inebriated stupor was… quiet. Non-violent. Better than the day he threw a teacup at my head. I'd ducked. It shattered against the wall, sprinkling shards of bone china onto our newborn son who lay sleeping in his bassinet next to me. Removing each tiny sliver and razor-thin flake from his tender face, my hands trembling with adrenaline, was the most careful work I have ever done. My own eyes blurry with tears, I worked around his – quickly, before he stirred and woke, causing more serious injury than just his tiny cuts, the kind that occur when broken glass hits you – usually on your lower legs, when you've dropped a glass on the floor all by yourself.

I was a dancer. We like to be barefoot – a high-stakes habit when you live with a thrower. Many household items were hurled my way by that former All-Star pitcher. Picture frames, car keys, wine glasses – whatever was within reach when the urge arose in him. Usually my instincts did not render a child the recipient as it happened that day. More often it was just me cornered in the kitchen, surrounded by broken glass, walking right across it to snatch up a baby before he came crawling or toddling to me, frightened, but willing to incur injury to get to his mother.

I thought about the day I heard his father's borrowed Ferrari rumbling and screeching into the parking lot of the bridal shop where my wedding dress was being altered. I was there with my sister, who was a bridesmaid. We were having fittings. My two young nephews were there as well. They were three and five years old at the time and excited to be ring bearers. Miserably he stormed into the establishment and into the dressing area, deeply concerned, outraged that the little boys might see me, his bride and therefore his property, in a state of undress.

My body, where my spirit lived. Mine, housing also both my brain and my ethics, none of which I could lay claim to at that time in my life.

The death of a lifelong friend was the beginning of a turning point for me. Everyone cried at Sharon's funeral, of course. She was beloved, funny, a devoted wife and mother, a cherished marker on our familiar landscape. I'd known her in church my entire childhood and camped with her and a small multi-family group of absolutely die-hard campers, twice a year, rain or shine, for several decades. No matter where else life took us, we reunited by our fire.

Everyone, that is, except for me. Campouts went like this during my first marriage: We'd either not go at all, no real discussion required because it was just obvious that we wouldn't, or we'd establish that we were going, but as I readied our belongings, made a list, and organized sleeping bags and flashlights, the atmosphere would change. He became so tormented, so harassing and vindictive, so belittling and threatened by my love for anyone other than him that the trip and I were ruined before we could even load the car. Some Mother's Days were like this as well. I'd show up at the country club for brunch with our extended families, wrecked. Make-up long cried away, eyes swollen, chest blotchy and voice shaky, trying to smile and make things nice for everyone with potted plants as offerings.

Sometimes, though, we'd arrive at the campout intact. We'd set things up with the best of intentions and enjoy ourselves, only to leave shortly thereafter. His demands would become so paranoid and isolating that we weren't able to leave our own campsite easily, and others didn't know how to approach us. Oftentimes I was grateful when people stayed away. That way they'd never know he had threatened to hurt them, either physically or by saying horrible, mean things. That way he couldn't make good on those detailed promises to me.

Everyone cried at Sharon's funeral with hearts broken in a way only suicide can break them, creating a backwardness to everything that remains forever. Everyone cried, but not like me. I cried so hard and for so long I couldn't hear the sermon or eulogy. My devastation embarrassed me; it felt disrespectful to her bereft family, and I excused myself to find a quiet hallway. Even there I couldn't recover my composure, sounding like an animal I've never heard before. My disappointment and frustration felt outrageous, supremely unfair, and more than I could accept. Years lost. Time – days, hours I could have had with my friend, disallowed for no reason, and I had agreed to all of it. I had soothed and obeyed, lied and covered up, scrambled to calm, and missed out on love for what would soon become the last time. The pain and remorse I felt that day grew into defiance, and that defiance took hold in me one night at my brother's wedding reception.

It had been the sweetest wedding, held in an old loft space lined with benches they'd built themselves. Their tiny dog, Sebastian, carried the rings down the aisle right on cue. We paraded to the reception afterward. Happily we marched across the square, a beautiful day in downtown Bloomington, Indiana, with my brother and his lovely bride laughing and leading the way. Everyone had balloons and absolutely nothing, nothing, was wrong – until two songs into the reception. I had danced to the first song, a current one, with my family while he sat and watched. That song was followed by a Frank Sinatra tune, older, swingy, though I can't remember the name of it. My father was near me. We automatically grabbed hands and had that dance together. I loved it. I'll never forget the life in his body, the joy emanating from him at the knowledge of his son's happiness and companionship. Years of hard work paying off, I suppose, with a major sacrament and meaningful event going well for all to keep as a memory.

Well, that did it. I had danced with someone else — my father, mind you, but that's not the point. Or maybe it was. And to Frank Sinatra of all people! He fancied himself worthy of that era — swanky, elegant, charming, and talented — all things he sort of was, actually. He adored everything Rat Pack.

Suddenly it was time to leave. Only two songs in, family from all over the country gathered in a single space for just one night, and we were leaving the reception. "You should have known better!" he screamed. I looked around the loud, lively room. I saw not only my precious, patient family, but some of our campout friends as well. I saw Sharon's widower, and my children running around, shirttails out, waving and sword fighting with peacock feathers they'd slipped from the centerpieces I had helped create. "No," I said, "I'm staying. But you can leave if you want to."

In times prior I would have begged him to forgive me, to calm down, to please, please stay and not be angry. There would have been storming about and something broken, a cut or bruises somewhere on my body from having been in the path of the storm. But not this time. I turned my back to him, braced myself for what might come and tried to dance again. I breathed in the strength and love in the numbers and presence of my family and friends and looked straight forward, ready for whatever he chose to do with his 6'2" 240 lb frame. He left. He took our car seat and diaper bag with him and drove back to Indianapolis.

I had a wonderful night. I talked, laughed, and danced the night away without shedding a single tear! Actually, that's not true — the toasts had us all a soppy mess, but that's different. As the evening wore on, my youngest ones curled up on couches the way they do when it's all too good to leave just yet, but too late for eyes that have grown heavy; the time for retreating to a cozy spot, to be covered by a man's suit coat and lulled by the music and familiar voices carried on the air, by the sound of ice clinking in glasses and the rise and fall of laughter, drifting off to sleep under low, sparkling lights while those who care for you keep watch. With help from the women in my family we managed the children's care without any gear. It was a first step. I kept with me a longstanding sorrow for the man who simply couldn't be at peace, but I also chose to love life.

Around that same time my daughter got her first period. It was a Sunday, and we were at church. We sat on the sidewalk outside of CVS afterward and talked, pausing life for a moment as childhood was edging past us, day by day. As I sat with her I began to realize that I was running out of time, that my children would grow up and leave home thinking their life was…what? Normal? They would become adults having never seen a better way to live than this. Others I loved would die at some point, and, if I stayed, I would spend my entire life accommodating wasteful wishes, constantly scanning the horizon for trouble, and missing everything I needed and wanted to do.

I was walking down the first floor gallery in our home one afternoon not long after that. I passed the library and stopped, backing up to look inside the room. Emma was there with her father, sitting just near enough for her level of comfort. They were having a conversation, which was a very odd sight. She was saying more than usual, and he had not yet dismissed her. In fact, he was smiling while he listened. And then I saw the glass of scotch in his hand and heard his slurry, slow responses. I realized with sickness moving through my body that she had figured something out – that the time to enjoy her father, to have some sort of warm experience with him and to receive attention from him was when he was not sober.

And that was it. The guilt I felt was crippling. I was going to break the promise I had made to him. "In sickness and in health" was going to kill my spirit and any growth or decency I hoped to have as a woman, as a mother, as a daughter, sister, and friend. I had let the children become "accidentally" hurt during his suspiciously rough play too many times, waiting and praying for conversation and sacrifice to heal and transform him. He was an untreated alcoholic with raging personality disorders, challenges he would not bow down to and accept. Through at times flailing and misguided efforts, I found my path and a way free of the syndrome that ruled our lives, leaving behind a beautiful old estate and a retirement, as well as a husband and provider.

I did not, as was feared by those who love me, end up dead in our woods. I did not, and I still haven't.

Those memories visit me occasionally. However, logging out of Facebook, my thoughts turned ultimately to my life now, to my husband, Terence, the love of my life, whose late introduction gave me time to begin living wholly and independently, learning to negotiate my experiences in the world with the Complex PTSD I had inevitably acquired over the years.

Terence honors my body and my soul. He sometimes struggles to honor his own after a childhood that included, along with its beauty, violence and neglect at the hands of relatives, as well as having battled a high school wrestling-induced eating disorder. We each struggle, but our life together is an intimate dance in which we nurture each other's divinity, finding sacrament therein.

I know his wounds, and he knows mine. We're like a couple of retired NFL players, best friends who made early legacies on different teams. We know where the repetitive hits affected each of us – one with a cranky, difficult shoulder that brings the other around to help finish painting a granddaughter's playhouse, and one with a bad knee that dictates a tendency to pass by the stairs and take the long way around to find the elevator together. I like it. I like it a lot. We are sanctuary for one another. Old souls in young bodies.

We went "off grid" for a while in order to find and build this sacred place and to learn to live as a family of seven. We re-booted and rebuilt our connections to loved ones with greater purpose and care, doing so as husband and wife. Perspective with a couple of friendships shifted to accommodate this, friendships that presented too challenging a dynamic for the spiritual sanctity of our marriage. That has been, and still is difficult to navigate, and sometimes sad, but the thought of never living with honor for ourselves, never holding protected space in which to give and receive love respectfully, to grow and heal, is infinitely more painful.

Recently we applied to become licensed to care for foster infants. We met for lunch one day at Cracker Barrel and filled out our paperwork, plates of eggs, bacon, and pancakes and stacks of papers between us. For us, ordering eggs take priority somewhere near the top of, well, a lot of things in life, and is a process that requires both pause and due consideration, mine always scrambled with cheddar or not at all — unless rye toast is offered on the menu, in which case I'll eat them cheese-less, but restaurants in Indiana don't always offer rye toast — and his either over easy or over medium, depending on a feeling he gets from our server. That feeling is determined after speculative, in-depth conversation between them, a ritual that establishes definitions of terms and degrees of "done" as they each understand them, at times slowly circling around the question, "But will the whites be see-through?" Like a gunslinger he watches every gesture to divine truth and expectations regarding the situation at hand. Our server begins bobbing his or her head emphatically with big encouraging eyes, while Terence's narrow and probe in effort to predict the likely outcome of the yolks and the quality of the working relationship this person has with the cook, wondering just exactly what was written down on his order (without actually asking to look at it), his head beginning to bob in sync, too. There is silence for a moment as a profile is created in his mind, their eyes locked, and he finally surrenders his fate to a duo that may or may not possess the perspicacity necessary for these eggs to turn out as he hopes.

I don't think I could love a person more.

"Okay. Okay, let's do it," he concluded with our waitress that day, protocol once again exercised. "Thank you." Eyes on my phone all the while, perusing emails I'd already read, I asked, "You good?"

"Yeah," he said, taking a cleansing breath, "I mean, sure, I think so. Yes," and giving me a reassuring nod, returned to his papers. Imagining a flipped over restaurant high chair beside us cradling a baby in a pumpkin seat, I combined two stacks of papers to create space for a second plate of redone eggs to arrive later.

The forms contained background checks, FBI and criminal history — all of it, as well as personal questions about our relationship. Working my way through, I got to the question, "How would you describe your sexual relationship?" I noticed the answers ranged from "Highly compatible" on down the line to something I can't recall. The list included lesser and lesser descriptions that I barely bothered skimming because they wouldn't have applied. When I read the choice, "Somewhat compatible", my eyes flicked back to "Highly".

Thinking about his face, warm and close to mine, and the shape of him – the scruffy line of his jaw and most tender eyes, a cloudy blue, and the way his mouth is delicious to me, the way he smells like home and feels like magic, his forehead pressing closer and finding a place where the ins and outs of my heart and mind and other things are kept, the breath of his voice right there, low and full of intention, and knowing so sweetly where we take that, I made my mark. I needed consider no further. I smiled at the sight of my flourishing checkmark, squirming a little in my seat, knowing without looking right where he'd placed his smaller, left-handed "x" on his form.

And you know, the man does possess a fair amount of diligence, undeniably. It's pretty much required for those who work at a doctoral level as he does. But try as he might – and believe you me, he's been pursuing the subject with concentration for several years now – he hasn't found a single thing wrong with my vagina.

Memories… Like the day I felt fun and feminine, deciding that a ruffled swimsuit and rain boots were kind of artsy and had let the camera snap away. "Ruined breasts" and all, a chapter of my life was preserved on film. I knew that my daughter as well as my four sons would be affected in some way by my self-acceptance, by my own celebration of just what-all this body has accomplished, and I knew that it mattered. Indeed, it mattered that I had *enjoyed* it. Those photos, along with others, would later be given to an agent and used to cast me in commercials and an educational film for the Discovery Channel.

Maybe I'll link the memory of that day together with other moments when I felt lovely regardless, just regardless, and, along with memories of all the exquisite days of a "highly compatible" marriage, a union that feels for all the world like prayer, I'll make them into a silvery, delicate chain to wear dangling from my wrist.

And when someone offers me a compliment, saying, "What a beautiful piece of jewelry! Who designed that?" I won't say, "Oh, it's just costume. It's nothing." Instead I'll say, "Thank you, I made it myself. And it's real."

Maybe another day I'll even paint my fingernails.

About the Author
Jeanne Louise Mayhue

Jeanne Louise Mayhue can be contacted at
jlmayhue.inquiry@outlook.com
or you can 'Follow' her on Facebook: Jeannie Mayhue

What did you want to be when you were eight years old?

When I was eight years old I wanted to be a mother. By then I'd already ascertained that this declaration wasn't what my public would consider satisfactory. I was born in the 70's, after all, and a lot of work had been done to make it so that little girls could think "bigger" thoughts, so I told people I wanted to become an airline pilot. I really tried to feel that way, too. I played it out. I spent my time singing and dancing around the house and yard and playing with dolls, waiting to grow older, but when asked what I wanted to be when I grew up, I'd tip my head back to look up into people's faces and try on the answer, "I want to be a pilot. I'd like to fly airplanes." Five beautiful children later, I am what I genuinely wanted to be then, among other things – namely one striving to be a spiritual resource for those I'm blessed to encounter, and writing some, still singing and dancing around the house, rather joyfully.

Anything else?

My deepest gratitude to everyone whose voice is spoken in this piece, and to all who have been witness to these events in my life and the lives of my children. Thank you for your presence then and during the better days that came, and have yet to come.

Two

"I dwell in possibility."

—Emily Dickinso

AN ORGASMIC BIRTH
by Tara Kilbane Dixon

I should have known something was up when I was sitting cross-legged in the center of sculptor Richard Serra's "Torqued Ellipse". The tilted, cylindrical steel walls of his work provided the perfect membrane between me and the outer world. I felt protected by the richly patinated surfaces holding the tension within my body. I felt like I was in a giant womb.

The baby had dropped. My belly was big and heavy, grazing the floor of the Dia Foundation's gallery. I absorbed the coolness of the poured cement floor through my stretch maternity pants and remember saying to my gallery-going friend, "I don't want to move. I could give birth right here in Chelsea." I didn't realize it at the time, but this last day of April, 1998, would be my last experience of art as a non-mother.

The due date was eight days away, May 8th. I felt tension in my lower back, and I was weary. It felt like I was dragging a ton of bricks from my sacrum. I would learn later that this was called "back labor".

My husband, who spent a great deal of time on airplanes, was in Dallas that day. Later, we would also learn that he had no business traveling so close to the due date.

"Hey, Bey."

"Hey," I remember exhaling into our cordless phone in our East Village tenement third-floor walk-up.

"Just finished up here in Dallas – checking in. How are you?"

"I'm fine," I remember answering almost automatically.

I told him about the rounded slabs of rusted steel I had found refuge in earlier that day. For whatever reason, I refrained from saying my back

19

ached. And that I was exhausted. I was used to going things alone and being stoic. In many ways, I was disconnected from my body.

When he asked if he should go on to Vancouver, I told him to go.

An hour after his plane took off, I started to bleed. When he landed in Vancouver, he got a message from the airline that his wife had gone to the hospital. My roommate from college lived around the corner from me, and she came over, finished packing my bag and took me to Beth Israel Hospital. The next twelve hours, I would labor with her by my side. We had pulled many all-nighters together while in school. This was definitely the most memorable, and what we were preparing for was more daunting then any final exam.

As my husband traversed the country on the next flight to LaGuardia, he and I had brief conversations from my hospital room phone to the airplane phone. These continued until the contractions got too intense and rapid. I imagined listening to Neil Young's "Harvest Moon". Making a mixed tape for the birth was another thing that had somehow gone by the wayside. Just as I had to visualize my partner being there in that hospital room instead of in a metal capsule rushing through space, I stretched to listen to the non-existent, soothing notes of this song.

From my hospital bed I could see a sliver of the city. By some chance the view was directly aligned with the Chrysler Building. I looked at this iconic structure for inspiration as my friend fed me ice chips and my cervix dilated. During the contractions, I counted the art deco triangles and imagined drawing the building in my mind. When I was offered the epidural, I refused it. I wanted my whole body to be present for this experience.

"PUSH!" my doctor shouted. One triangle. Two triangles. Three triangles. Four triangles … I would never be able to look at the Chrysler Building in the same way.

"He's crowning!" I remember hearing. We had found out the sex of our baby but had kept it a secret. He even had been named for several months. This was the big moment, and his father was probably somewhere over New Jersey. I had long since left my human existence. I remember wailing and groaning, connecting to my animal-self. Something wondrous happened as I felt this body exiting my vaginal canal. My wailing began to harmonize into music. This music took the form of exhalations of sound that were reminiscent of opera. My whole body was pulsing and throbbing like a musical instrument. A sweet rush of ecstasy emanated from my clitoris. I felt tingling in my mouth, fingers and toes. I continued to sing as my body did the same. This full-body smile faded in slow motion as my son was brought to my chest.

It was recorded that he came out of me at 8:22 am. His father remembers looking at his watch as the plane made contact at exactly the same time. Somehow this synchronicity and the orgasmic bliss made everything all right. No matter who was present and where it took place, a new life had begun, and he came in with a song.

About the Author
Tara Kilbane Dixon

What did you want to be when you were eight years old?

An artist.

If you could give one piece of advice to your younger self about your orgasm, what would it be?

That it is a conduit for freedom and creativity.

If your orgasm had a voice, what would your orgasm say to you about the piece you wrote for this book?

It would be very proud. It would say, "Good for you for sharing this beauty with the world!"

THREE

Silent Seat

When you finally take
your calm and silent seat
on the throne
of your own heart
everything begins to fall into
it's proper place
because
You
have.

—from *Make Me Your Own,*
by Tosha Silver

DEAR BETSY...
by Betsy Blankenbaker

Almost immediately after the release of *Autography of an Orgasm*, my book based on my five years of researching orgasm, something unexpected happened. I started receiving letters from women – and a few men – who saw bits of themselves in my story. I'd known some of these people for years, and just as they were surprised by my revelations that I'd spent a great deal of my life shut down from an enjoyable sensual life, I was surprised to learn that they had also experienced shame or dissatisfaction around their bodies and sex. Like me, they had been hiding behind their secrets and pretending that everything was okay.

One woman in her seventies wrote to me that she'd been sexually dysfunctional her entire life after experiencing abuse when she was young. She added that although she was glad I was able to recover and heal from the sexual trauma, she felt it was too late for her. I disagree. Dr. Christiane Northrup writes in her book, *Goddesses Never Age*, "You are sitting on a throne of gold, the fountain of youth, and it is your erotic anatomy. Explore it and get to know it." Your clitoris has 8,000 nerve endings – more than any other part of your body – and they're present at birth and death. They were not put there to be ignored. It is never too late.

I received another letter from a sixteen year old girl who had sneaked my book from her mother's purse and read it cover to cover. She thanked me for writing about all the ways I gave myself away and felt damaged from a young age. She said she had, too. She thanked me for writing that, despite the damage, I finally remembered that my body was still sacred. And she now believes she can, too.

Some people shared their stories privately. Many more asked for advice on what to do next so they could start feeling their orgasm and more of their lives. I'm including two of the letters here. I've changed the writers' names for privacy, but they did give me permission to share their letters.

> *Dear Betsy,*
>
> *Thank you for writing your book. Your courage has encouraged me to start the healing that I know I desperately need after rape in college and disconnection from my body. My mother was raped, too, and she never spoke about it.*
>
> *How do you let go of so much shame? How do you enjoy a body that has brought you more pain than you care to admit?*
>
> *—Ella*

Ella,

There is no one solution for everyone. We are all different, so it's really important to listen to your inner wisdom. I know at the start of my orgasm research, when I committed to the thirty days of stroking my clitoris just to feel whatever came up, I really had to pay attention to each stroke, listen to my body's feedback, and make the tiniest adjustments to try and feel even more. It was me becoming the expert on myself. I stopped judging myself and was instead just curious.

How do you get better at listening to your body? One thing that really helped me was taking Qoya classes. I'm not sure where you live, but you can check the website (www.loveqoya.com) for local classes and retreats and to see if it interests you. There are even free videos on the site. The classes are part dance and part yoga (no levels and no experience required). A Qoya class is designed to help you remember how your body likes to move by paying attention to the feeling in your body. I remember being a kid on the playground and only doing the things I loved during recess because they made me feel good. As a child, I wouldn't repeat a movement over and over again if it didn't feel good in my body. As adults, we shouldn't either. During every Qoya class, we spend one song shaking every part of our body. We shake as a way to reset on a cellular level and to move the stuck energy through us. It's using movement as medicine. Qoya was as important to me as the thirty days of stroking my clit to feel my orgasm again because it revealed to me how to listen to my body, and with each class, I feel like I liberate a little more of my authentic self. And the classes made it easier for me to listen to my body when I was doing the more intimate research to feel my orgasm.

I also recommend spending three to four minutes every morning and night giving yourself a massage. Put on a favorite song while you do it. I call it the *Water Blessing Massage Ritual*, because our bodies are over 70% water, and the self-massage is a way to imprint love on every part of your body. Remember when I wrote in *Autobiography of an Orgasm* about my nearly dead orchid coming back to life when I told it I loved it every day for thirty days? That is what this massage does – it sends the message of love to every cell. Imagine rubbing gratitude or love into every area of your body. Your cells will carry that message through the day or through the night as you sleep. It may sound like a corny thing to do – like telling a plant you love it! – and it may be uncomfortable at first. Do it like your life depends on it, though, because it does. Our vaginas and brains are connected, and when we cut off feeling from all the nerve endings in our genitals, we deny our brains the signals that nourish our bodies, stimulate our creativity and give us a sense of wellbeing. Try it for seven days, and then extend it to forty.

Commit to stroking your clitoris for fifteen minutes a day. Consider this, too, a sacred ritual, like a prayer honoring your body. I call this the *Sacred Orgasm Ritual*. Begin the ritual with a few minutes of sending deep breaths all the way into your womb and pelvis. This sends fresh, clean oxygen to the area and increases blood flow. Inhale into your womb and then exhale the breath through your genitals ten times. Then, inhale hum with every exhalation ten times. Next, trace ten circles around the outer lips of your vulva. Take it slowly, and notice whether you prefer a lighter touch or a firmer one. And then begin stroking your clit for fifteen minutes without any attachment to results. Your only goal is to feel whatever you are feeling and then make adjustments to see if you can feel even more.

I think many of us had mothers and grandmothers who experienced sexual trauma and never spoke about it or healed from it. Some of our great-great-grandmothers were even burned for it.

When we don't choose to heal, the shame and disillusionment get passed on to the next generation. We have to be braver than our mothers were, because we can't afford to pass this on to our daughters. And we can't afford to live less than fully in our bodies in this lifetime. If we do, we continue the cycle of abuse, except instead of the men who raped us or the boys who assaulted us in college, we become our own abusers by not choosing to heal and recover. It's a choice we make every day when we look in the mirror and see ourselves with love or see ourselves with judgment.

Releasing the shame and enjoying your body after the abuse you experienced requires you to be a tiny bit braver than you have been before. It's a choice. It's worth it.

I know you can do it. I did.

—Betsy

Dear Betsy,

I am reading your wonderful book and feel compelled to reach out to you. I am 45 and just beginning the journey of healing from a past that is very similar to yours. I share so many of the same experiences as you — it's interesting to hear my story in your story: early abuse by a neighbor, lack of boundaries, abortion, lack of sexual zeal, divorce, lack of emotional and physical feeling, being disconnected from orgasm, faking it, etc. I'm sure many other women share these experiences, too. Thank you for opening up and being so honest about what you experienced and how you healed. Because of your book I am now very inspired to fully commit to my own healing and am so excited to get on with it! I don't really know my next steps — it would seem logical to try some of the things you did. If you have any advice, I would love to hear it. Thank you, dear one, for lighting the way.

—Marilyn

Marilyn,

You are not alone. We are not alone.

According to recent statistics, at least one in five women has either experienced sexual assault and/or is "orgasmically challenged" (as an article in *The U.K. Sunday Times* referred to me). At first, I rejected the "orgasmically challenged" label, but then I remembered, there is nothing wrong with us! We've just received a lot of misinformation about our bodies. The truth is, once I understood how my body worked, my orgasm flowed freely. The bigger issue was feeling safe enough in my body to allow myself to feel again. My body was not "orgasmically challenged"; my mind and thoughts were the obstacles. Once I committed to listening to my body, I also committed to learning everything I could about how I was wired. I spent plenty of years letting myself be wired for shame and depression. Now, I was choosing to understand how my body was wired for pleasure, and I was going to practice in the same way I committed to anything that really mattered. I found that it's possible to heal yourself through orgasm when it's practiced with love and intention, rather than the quick 'getting off' climaxes that last only a few seconds.

Another important shift in beliefs about orgasms is to remember that your orgasm begins with the first sensations you feel in your body. The sensations, your orgasm, is your sensual being sending you messages, asking you to pay attention. You will continue to orgasm as you listen to your body to find the places to touch, stroke and massage that expand your orgasm. Every touch is a chance to go further into – or away – from your orgasm. That's why it's important to practice so you become the expert on your body and your orgasm.

There is orgasm and there is climax. They are not the same. Sometimes, your orgasm will include climaxing (what we used to believe was our orgasm). But it's never about the climax. It's about following the path of your orgasm so you stay present with yourself and only do the next touch or move that honors your orgasm. I wonder what would happen to women if we devoted the same amount of time trying to understand our bodies and serving our orgasm as we did to getting our nails done, or going to the gym or watching Netflix?

29

Our brain is designed to achieve states of ecstasy and bliss. We can get there through movement, like dance and Qoya classes; breathing and yoga; prayer and meditation; and through orgasm. All of these techniques feed our brains and have the potential to connect us with a higher state of consciousness. All of these tools put our bodies in balanced states of wellness for ultimate healing.

One woman wrote to me after reading my book to ask why I needed to have so much sex as I was healing my vagina. This is what I know: my commitment to healing had to be as big as the original damage and the years of ignoring myself. I couldn't just take a class or swallow a pill or read a book and get better. I committed to feeling my orgasm (and my body and my life) in the same way an athlete commits to training for an event. And none of the early stuff I did felt very good, because feeling the tingling sensations in my body meant I also had to feel and remember the pain again (instead of just shutting it all out, like I had done for years). I also know that when I finally committed to feeling more of my orgasm (and the climaxes that came without trying) the rest of my life started feeling better, too. Now, I understand the science behind it, but at the time I thought it was just coincidence.

I actually did most of the research in private, by myself. In *Autobiography of an Orgasm*, I wrote about the courses I took and then how it went with men I dated, but the real healing happened as I got to know my body and fell in love with myself. Even after I published the book, I looked back on the final chapter with self-judgment for sleeping with the guy on the first date (especially because we didn't continue to see each other more than a few dates). But then I remembered what was truly healing in that experience – being back in Indiana, lying in grass (as I had at the beginning of the book after I was abused), and making my own choices. I was setting my own sensual path instead of letting someone else chart it for me.

Just as I recommended to Ella (see above), consider doing the *Water Blessing Massage Ritual* and the *Sacred Orgasm Ritual* every day for thirty or forty days. Take a Qoya class or a dance class. Walk in nature. Take a writing class or sign up for Laura Davis's free writing prompts at www.lauradavis.net. Be mindful of your daily habits, because our habits

30

become our rituals. I invite you to look for more meaningful rituals that honor your body as sacred.

My friend Rochelle Schieck said, "Imagine if the way you move your body is how you talk to God." In researching your body and your orgasm, I would add, "Imagine if how you choose to honor your body (and your orgasm) is how you talked to God." Whatever God or Source you believe in, the fact is we were born with our bodies wired for pleasure, so why would we ignore that chance to have the conversation?

Choose your path. Follow your curiosity. Listen to your body.

We are our own best healers.

—Betsy

About the Author
Betsy Blankenbaker

www.betsyblankenbaker.com

Six Things I'm Most Proud of in 2015

1. I now find the sacred in the darkest moments of life – those moments that used to take me out for days or weeks because I didn't want to deal with anything confrontational or uncomfortable. Now I find soulfulness in sitting with the darkness instead of ignoring it, because I've seen that there's always something beautiful waiting for me as soon as I go through it instead of pushing it away.

2. I love that when I follow my curiosity, I always discover a person, a place or an experience that makes life even better.

3. I'm proud that I am not caught up in trying to manifest the next best version of my life. My focus is on awakening more deeply into the present moment and offering my life to be of service for the highest good. And to feel more of everything, including my orgasm.

4. I am proud of my collection of friends around the world who truly leave me feeling like a better version of myself when I spend time with them.

5. I quit ballet and all dance lessons when I was a child because I was told I was not good. Now, over forty years later, I teach Qoya, which combines dance, yoga and sensual movement. Qoya allows us to remember how it feels to enjoy being in our bodies. For more information on classes and retreats: www.loveqoya.com.

6. I love seeing my four grown children making a difference in the lives of others. I've witnessed each of them quietly contributing to someone who needed extra support. I learned to help others as a child because I grew up with parents who gave back, and I love seeing this important part of my parents' legacies living on in my own children.

FOUR

*"Your problem is how you are going to spend this one
and precious life you have been issued. Whether you're
going to spend it trying to look good and creating the
illusion that you have power over circumstances, or
whether you are going to taste it, enjoy it and find out
the truth about who you are."*

—Anne Lamott

IN THE BELLY OF THE GODDESS
by Maggie Marie Genthner

My mom and dad had a passionate relationship. I was always told that I rode in on a wave of bliss. I am the daughter of two Buddhists who built a retreat center in the Midwest of the United States. Our house was often flooded with monks, prominent Zen teachers and meditation students.

The adults chanted *The Heart Sutra* daily.

> "Avalokitesvara Bodhisattva
> when practicing deeply the Prajna Paramita
> perceives that all five skandhas are empty
> and is saved from all suffering and distress."
>
> [heard over a wooden mok-tok, a metronome – cluck...
> cluck...cluck...cluck...]
>
> "All Buddhas depend on Prajna Paramita
> and attain Anuttara Samyak Sambodhi.
> Therefore know that Prajna Paramita
> is the great transcendent mantra,
> is the great bright mantra,
> is the utmost mantra,
> is the supreme mantra."

"Mommmm... Daaaaaddd.... ahhhhhhhh!" I yelled as I ran through the meditation center, interrupting the silence of the adults. I was five years old and my little brother was almost three. Nearly out of breath, I panted, "We...uh... just saw...uh... snake. It was rattling and it tried to get us!" I gasped for air.

My little brother and I had decided to go pick blackberries by ourselves that day and had stumbled upon a rattlesnake nest; the mother snake was furious. In my first ever heroic effort, I flung myself to face her as she rattled. I screamed to my little brother to run back to the meditation hall, and then I quickly ran behind him.

In my own life I have realized that commitment to spiritual practice is not a safeguard; it doesn't guarantee that we will always be free from harm. In fact, it can open up a whole new landscape – full of unknown dangers, both internal and external.

I remember the feelings distinctly, but I barely remember the details of another incident. It hurt. Badly. Our parents were working, and I was at home with my brother, a baby-sitter and some older neighborhood boys. Suddenly, for no reason, I was kicked in my vulva. I felt the jerk of my body, heel to pubic bone – it was like an electric shock. Something told me that I needed to keep this a secret. I thought I would get someone in trouble if I told, and then it would really not be safe. I don't remember who did it or why; there were too many in the room to assign responsibility to one. I do remember wanting to hide, and I couldn't believe someone would cause me so much pain. Why did they gang up on me?

Later, when I went to look at my body in the bathroom, I pulled down my underwear and saw that I was bruised, black and blue. I was sore and swollen, but I pulled my pants back up and zipped them, keeping my secret to myself.

After the kick, things in my life were less than ok. At school that week, I held my belly and complained of feeling sick. The bruise disappeared pretty quickly, but the feeling of what happened lingered. I didn't have a word for it, but I felt that I had been punished, and I hadn't done anything wrong.

"What's your sister doing?" a neighborhood boy asked my brother. "She stays in the basement all day. She's the Princess of the Basement."

"Is she a lesbian or something?" another boy said.

I escaped their bullying by staying away from them. I sat behind the glowing screen of my computer and wrote.

In middle school, I had a posse of girls whom I led to wear glitter and listen to the Spice Girls. That was our female liberation. At other times, I was shy and sensitive. I was growing up fast, but I felt pretty empty inside. I would sometimes steal bottles of wine. I never got drunk, but I knew that's what people did to relax, so I did it, too.

My parents decided to send me to a Catholic high school. I never understood why. We were Buddhist, not Catholic. Barely able to navigate socially, I was thrown to even bigger wolves – coaches recruiting football players and giving them steroids, and a repressed thirty year-old religious teacher who told us he was a virgin and that we shouldn't have sex outside of marriage while simultaneously hitting on us. You could feel the soap opera rumbling under the school, and yet the buildings and grounds were well-funded.

One day in a biology class, a guy I kind of liked decided to stick his foot in my crotch during a lecture. I found myself feeling both angry at him and slightly turned on by the attention because I had been very attracted to him. His name was Tom; he was a baseball player, and he liked me. He always invited me to come see him practice.

"Do you like that?" he whispered as he felt me deeper. "You look like you do." I smiled and avoided the question.

By sophomore year, I decided to leave the country for boarding school in England. The school itself was in a large white mansion in the middle of sheep pastures and sprawling cedar trees. I met teenagers from all over the world. We grew our own food, set our own curriculum and started the day meditating together for fifteen minutes before breakfast. On weekends I travelled to London, where I walked around with friends in the pulse of the metropolitan city.

"Brad, I love you forever," I exclaimed as I kissed my first boyfriend in the streets of Soho. We were fourteen years old. A street performer cycled past us and said, "This, folks, is young love."

An eccentric French woman was my first Hatha yoga teacher. In one class, she told us to close our eyes, and we followed her meditation through the English countryside along dirt paths. We all cooed and called as we navigated our way together, holding onto a shoulder, or a finger, stumbling on a rock or traversing a ditch. The darkness wasn't scary because we were together in the unknown.

When I opened my eyes, we were in a field of purple-blue flowers. She had brought us to the edge of a bluebell forest. The smell was intoxicating, and my mind grew wild imagining little sprites and fairies making their homes in these tiny bell-shaped flowers. I left class grateful that my imagination had returned to me.

My yoga practice took on a whole new meaning for me after that. It was how I nourished my soul.

In England, I explored my sexuality with a French boy named Alfred. He always grabbed me, and it felt gross. Once, he wanted to see how many times we could have sex in one night before we left school for the holidays. He didn't look at me. He grunted and overwhelmed me with his sweaty, heavy body. I felt used. Thank God this experience was at the end of the term. I had two months to think about how bad it felt, and when I came back to school I finally broke up with him.

Later he asked me, "Did I ever hurt you?" I couldn't even reply. Years later, another girl confided to me that she'd also had a bad experience with him. I grew angry knowing that that was probably how he treated a lot of girls. And none of us spoke up.

I had my first orgasm with an older boyfriend named Martin when I was eighteen years old and still in secondary school. He was twenty-three. When it happened, we were on holiday at his home in Germany. He lit the room with candles. It felt like a shrine. My body felt fed by his touch. He was sitting cross-legged, and I was wrapped around him like statues I had seen of the Buddha and his consort.

I felt my vagina flood with warmth and intensity. My heart opened as my body melted. I felt so relaxed.

The power of the orgasm was intense. I was feeling new places in my body and heart. I was growing beyond the girl I had been, and yet being a woman didn't quite feel like something I was ready to own. At times with Martin, I found myself ambivalent about having someone touch me so deeply. One afternoon, while we were having sex, the condom broke. He didn't stop.

"Hey, what are you doing?" I said as he continued and ejaculated inside of me. He didn't answer.

I had felt so fertile and ripe. And I had trusted him. Now, I was so angry that he kept going when he knew the condom was not working. I prayed that I wasn't pregnant and then decided that wasn't enough. I took a morning after pill.

I didn't fall hard in love again until I met James. James was a poet with dark hair and eyes. We met and fell in love on a sunny day, while he was sitting on a bench in Boulder, Colorado. We had never met before, but we recognized each other. He asked me to go into an art gallery with him to look at glass vases that looked like vulvas. It was hard not to laugh at what looked so clearly like a clitoris in front of us. We went on elaborate art dates in the woods. He left me little notes:

"The lingering streams of light through trees as I searched for you."

He was crazy – not metaphorically, but diagnosed. He had, however, the most realistic outlook on the world of anyone I knew. He knew pain and was able to transcend it with words. We were not just lovers but great friends who cared deeply for each other. Everything in my college world broke open from his shadow. He was like looking into mystery. He infused me with mystery. And one day, out of the blue, he left for Korea. My heart broke.

It is hard to be the one who stays when love leaves. I was in Boulder, Colorado, at college with an ache. The winter was rough and blistery. I found myself frequenting a little hot yoga studio with an amazing view of the Rockies. For ninety minutes I was in 105 degrees and 40% humidity. It was the closest thing I had to a tropical vacation.

"Arms over your head... nice tight grip."

"Change."

"Savasana."

The repetition of the class was comforting. I could go on auto-pilot. It was like a trance. It felt good to strip away the day, to sweat and to forget about that man I missed so badly.

I noticed my body strengthening quickly – years of chronic back pain vanished over the course of three months as I began to open each vertebra. After seeing the transformation to increased flexibility in my body, I felt like I could do anything and change anything that appeared in my life as a limitation.

On the mat, I felt flexible and in control of my life. Off the mat, I was ready for a change. I decided to fly to Hawaii and attend a hot yoga teacher training.

I had been practicing every day and sometimes taking two or three classes. Training at altitude in Boulder had brought me to the peak of my physical fitness. Now I was ready to experience a bigger transformation on the inside.

I will never forget the first time I saw the guru. I was sitting on the floor during a lecture, surrounded by four hundred other yogis who were dedicating their lives for the next two months to his teaching program. On the first day, the guru walked into the hotel's yoga room wearing a black suit with shiny lapels. We were all in our yoga clothes.

"This was the smartest decision you have ever made," he boasted.

That sounded good, I thought. I had just left college to attend the guru's $10,000 yoga training, so I needed some reassurance that I was headed in the right direction.

"The farthest distance you will ever travel is the distance from your head to your heart," he continued.

I thought that was a beautiful teaching, and since I had always travelled and felt the need to flee, it gave me a sense of relief that at some point I would stop needing to travel, and I would find my home in my own heart.

During the first weeks of my teacher's training I met a man named Dave who loved yoga as much as I did. We enjoyed a great friendship and took many walks on the beach together, where we talked about opening a yoga studio someday. We enjoyed each other's company, but we were mostly focused on our yoga. We practiced memorizing the script that we would use to teach our classes.

"Inhale, lift up, drop your body down."

"Good job, you missed this part and this part," Dave said.

"Ok, thanks." And I would start again.

David saw learning the script as honoring the lineage and the guru. He described it as a transmission, slowly layering patterns of the words throughout his brain. I, however, wasn't ready to fully embrace this man as a guru. I had not been looking for a guru.

Nine weeks later, when I graduated from the teacher training, I had definitely changed – for one, I was carrying about five extra pounds of muscle. My jeans no longer fit over my quads, and I had cut off all my hair because the constant heat in the yoga room fried my curls.

My last encounter with the guru was during the four hundred person graduation. The ceremony consisted of a talk by Bishnu Ghosh, my guru's teacher. He spoke about the amazing benefits of yoga to unlock the keys to the kingdom of health. After I was handed my teaching certificate, I was then herded onto stage to have my picture taken with the guru. I looked young and had a great big beaming smile, but underneath the smoke and mirrors, something was missing. I didn't really feel the inner transformation I had hoped for.

"You look like a different person!" my friend screamed at me when I walked into her studio in my hometown. I had been through a lot; it was the most intense nine weeks of my life. I now had permission to teach, but becoming a teacher seemed like a daunting task.

I tried to go back to school in Boulder, but eventually I decided to put everything into becoming a better yoga teacher, so I moved to Oregon to live with Dave, my friend from Hawaii.

Dave and I spent the majority of 2008 to 2011 traveling together while he competed in and won several national yoga competitions. Sometimes I would be invited to teach by myself, and we would be apart for a few months. I would spend all my extra time on the mat, training. One day, during a backbend, my head went between my legs like a contortionist. I fell in love with back-bending.

I was becoming a very successful yoga teacher in this lineage with plans to open my own studio, but I still disliked teaching from the guru's script. Everything was about the script, and the script didn't help me understand the poses deeply, so I felt frustrated. I felt inauthentic, like a robot, teaching from a piece of paper. Other teachers raved about the script; I hated it. But I loved the practice. My favorite senior teacher didn't say one word of the script. She taught love, stillness, and breath.

Dave and I were invited to L.A. to train at our guru's studio. When we arrived, the guru greeted Dave with a wink and then pulled me in closer to his body for a hug. It felt incredibly awkward, but never creepy, more like a grandfather giving me a hug.

The guru said few words but always seemed delighted to see us. We thought he was great, and we really loved the yoga practice he shared with us. Dave believed that he was communicating to him in his dreams. I didn't feel the same connection, but for the most part I liked teaching and traveling, and I credited my ability to have those experiences to our teacher, because he invented the system that we lived and breathed. I had a lot of appreciation for him.

As I was getting established as a teacher, our yoga community was divided. The guru wanted all the studios that were teaching the sequence he created to pay him licensing fees. He started blacklisting so-called "copy-cat studios". Dave and I were loyal to the lineage, and we knew we wouldn't be teaching if it weren't for him. We were also grateful that the teacher training had brought us together.

"Hey, Maggie," Dave said one day. "I have an opportunity for us. Mario, my roommate from teacher training, just invited us to Bali to teach for a whole year."

"No way!" I said. "We've got to go. This is a once in a lifetime opportunity."

When Dave and I arrived in Bali, we were driven to our new home at the resort outside of Kuta, in the southern region. The resort was amazing. Even with jetlag, our eyes brightened and jaws dropped in awe of the tall wooden door with the intricate animal carvings, opening to marble floors with beautiful Asian sculptures.

"I have never been anywhere like this," I said, smiling, to Dave.

"Me either," he replied.

We were led down a pebbled walkway with exotic flowers, palms, and a large Ganesha statue. A few feet from our room was a pool with a swim up bar.

And then I saw her, the ocean, just five minutes away through the freshly combed sand.

"Rest up tonight. We'll meet in the morning," Mario said.

That night I ran to the ocean at sunset. The warm orange was lighting up the gentle waves. I was up to my knees in warm salt water, and I allowed Bali to enter me. I felt soft, feminine, and beautiful. All of the hard work brought me here — to magic. I was at the feet of the Goddess.

"Maggie, I didn't know that you were a mermaid," Dave said as he watched me. I winked at him. He and I had found paradise, and it was *shantik* (Balinese for "beautiful").

Bali is known as the island of the Gods and Goddesses. The people are some of the most open and friendly I have ever met. We enjoyed our time there, exploring Bali on mopeds and teaching yoga to Indonesian nobility.

Not too long after our arrival, we received bad news — the studio we were working for was not going to be certified because Mario had missed re-certifying with the yoga organization. We were committed to serving and honoring the lineage. We couldn't teach his yoga sequence at an unaffiliated studio. At some point the guru became our guru, and I felt an incredible loyalty to the practice. We stopped teaching, but we stayed on at our paradise. We took long rides through the jungle and rice fields. We surfed. And when our money ran out, we left. We flew back to Los Angeles for more training with our guru before returning to our home in Oregon.

We saw our guru again at the opening of a studio outside of Los Angeles. He and his wife were attending. He greeted us warmly. I remember that his shoes were shiny. At the time, I really liked his shoes and actually took a picture. Later, the Bukowski quote — Never trust a man with shiny shoes — would hold more meaning for me.

In 2011, Dave and I were invited to be on staff at the spring teacher training. We were both very honored and said yes to volunteering, happy to be of service to our guru's yoga lineage.

"You're going to be handling accommodations," a curly-haired Italian woman I knew from my own training said as she greeted me.

"Ok, that sounds good," I said, not really knowing what I was signing up for.

For the next nine weeks I was in charge of roommate disputes, unhappy yoga trainees, and bedbugs. Yes, there was a terrible infestation of bedbugs at the airport hotel. Later, I would start attending the guru by making him tea. It was a privilege to be of service to him.

"Are you kidding me, she said what?" I asked.

"Yes, Maggie, we need you to sit in on this roommate dispute." I looked in half-disbelief at another staff member, who would later become the guru's personal assistant. We were all eager to find our place in the organization, so we didn't complain.

"Try to keep them together in the room. We don't have an extra to put her in," I was told.

"OK," I said.

"Maggie, also, Boss needs his tea hotter." She and many other staff members liked to call the yoga master Boss. I always felt like they were half mocking him and half serious.

"He's yelling for you," she continued. I hurried off to find our guru in the lecture room with four hundred people.

"There's the little one," he said as I entered. "I want my tea to boil my balls."

"OK," I said and quickly turned to leave.

"See, she will make a good wife," he said as he pointed at me while the room full of people erupted in laughter.

It got to be a drill. The guru wanted something, and I was sent to fetch it. He would praise me. He would scold me. I thought it was all a game, a practice setting. This was a training, after all. It wasn't real life.

I stayed up at night watching Bollywood movies with him and the other staff members. Sleep deprivation was nothing. I was used to doing one hundred backbends a day. I knew it wasn't going to last forever, and I liked the feeling of hanging out with a man who was considered a yoga master among his followers. It reminded me of when I was a kid, and the Zen monks all came to my house. The monks were always lively, and we went to eat Chinese food. They gave me Korean money. My dad's teacher would hand me a bill and say, "When you grow up and go to Korea, you can buy a big cookie with this." It was probably the equivalent of fifty cents, but because it was a bill with several zeros, I always thought he was underestimating what I could buy.

The guru never gave me money. In fact, his organization wanted everything I did to be karma yoga, me giving back for the privilege of being in the yoga lineage. I was supposed to somehow prove my loyalty. Everything we did was about surrendering our egos while other people's egos grew in proportion to the influence they were given in the organization. Someone was keeping tabs. I never met that person (or the network) who determined who climbed and who was crushed.

There was an air of nonchalance in the inner circle of his room and staff. Initially, he wasn't outwardly creepy besides swearing and making people laugh, sometimes with inappropriate jokes during his lectures. I noticed he had a way of enforcing submission with his mercurial temper. It was so tiring to deal with his moods; most people just opted to try to read his mind so that he wouldn't correct them later and blow up. That worked about half of the time.

I became really good at reading the mood in the room when I had to do something for him. If he was in a bad mood, then I needed a lot of good luck to experience peace. His moods and rants were all seen as "the teaching".

People interpreted the experience as teaching us to go with the flow and to be ready and willing to surrender to the practice of yoga, which knew a greater balance than we could ever imagine.

After I finished the nine weeks, I visited my favorite senior teacher in San Francisco. She was helping me with my yoga poses.

"I worried about you down there," she said to me. "It's kind of like feeding lambs to the big bad wolf," she said.

"It was intense," I agreed. At this point, he had me psychologically bound, but he had not touched me.

In the fall of 2011, I was invited again to work for my guru at his teacher training studio in Los Angeles. Dave and I were at a rocky place in our relationship, wondering what our next step in life might be.

"Come down, work the teacher training and be with people who love you," said Anita, one of the staff members who worked at the office.

I felt raw. I didn't want my relationship to end, but we had some things we needed to work out, so Dave stayed behind in Oregon, and I flew down to L.A.

Even though I thought our teacher was ridiculous at times, I also saw him as wise, and I prided myself in taking care of him. Along with my daily responsibilities of buying food, making sure he had hot ginger tea at every lecture, setting up his various chairs and podiums, being available to the trainees for their questions, and giving feedback on the delivery of the script that they had to memorize, my guru began asking me to rub his feet. I did so, willingly. I was glad to help him feel better because he always complained of being in pain. We talked about my practice and my relationship with Dave. He asked about my mother. He took an interest in my life.

"We are a lot alike in the way we think," he said to me one day. "I want to give you a present. Do you know what transmission is?"

I nodded even though I didn't know what he had in mind. He was now my guru. Somehow life had led me to rely a great deal on this man and his yoga world. I trusted that he knew the next step in my training. But nothing happened after that inquiry. I wasn't invited to meditate with a group of his best students or given more guidance.

What happened next didn't make sense to me. One day when I was responsible to walk him to his room, while we were in the elevator, he spanked me on the butt, harder than just a tap. Surprised, I looked at him and rolled my eyes like it was a joke, but I didn't like the way he touched me. It hurt, and he had never touched me like that before.

A few days later, he took us all out to dinner. He liked this Chinese restaurant that did a la carte, and he was a fan of the crab legs. His Japanese girlfriend was beside him at dinner. We all knew that he had a girlfriend, but no one said anything. She was really handsome and noble. She wore a diamond on her left ring finger. We all assumed that she was an important person in his life. Her presence reassured me that whatever he was doing to me didn't have much meaning – he was just taking an opportunity to misbehave.

He began to leer at me. The attention made me feel uncomfortable. I was just a student he called "little one", and he didn't want anything from me, I told myself, but I was starting to feel disturbed by him. I kept up with my duties anyway.

He never liked to be alone and got really mad at the whole staff if anyone left him somewhere for a long period of time. I wondered if his odd behavior towards me – the spanking in the elevator and the frequent stares in my direction – was a cultural misunderstanding. Maybe he meant no harm. Why would he want to hurt me?

"Boss, I am here to walk you up to your room," I said.

"Let's go," he said. Before we left, I overheard him as he finished his conversation with his Indian friend. "I have no self-control," my guru said to his friend, laughing.

We took the elevator in awkward silence. As I was walking him down the long hallway, he seemed giddy and high, like he was intoxicated.

As we walked, he was humming under his breath.

We stopped at the door.

"OK," he said. "Now, you come inside and massage me to sleep."

"What?!" I said. In the past, I had only been asked to massage his feet as we talked.

He demanded my obedience with a stare and then pulled me into his room.

"You are just a bud, aren't you?" he said as he groped my breasts.

"Stop. I don't want this," I said. "You are married."

He kept pulling at me and trying to remove my clothes.

"No. Stop," I pleaded.

He continued. And then suddenly, he stopped.

"You can go now," he said. And I did.

Feeling like there was nobody I could talk to about this confusing experience, I just kept on with my duties. What was he going to do? I knew he was capable of pushing not only my boundaries but the boundaries of other people in the name of yoga, and I did not know how far he would go. The next morning when I went to the room to stock the kitchen, I knocked on his door and he told me to come in.

"You're an idiot for not wanting me," he said. And then he continued where he had stopped the night before. He tore at my clothes, grabbed my breasts and pulled himself on top of me until he got me naked.

I yelled at him to stop.

"This is not safe. You are not clear," I said. "What are you doing?"

But all he did was smirk. "I could have anyone. And now I want you."

He bound my legs up with his arms and forced me into a yoga pose.

Again, I screamed, "No! You are hurting me."

My words didn't stop him. His reply was, "It is supposed to hurt."

He pressed himself into me. I took a big gulp of air and he said, "You are a yogini, aren't you?"

And then, he raped me.

He did not ejaculate. "See, I did not get you pregnant."

Someone called him on his phone, and he was distracted for a moment. He started shouting into the phone, "I told you I was going to call you!"

I sneaked out and ran down the hallway to my room. I found my bed and just lay there motionless, not sure what had happened. I asked myself if I was at fault. Did I not make it clear enough that I did not want him to do that? I knew I had been clear, but now I didn't know where to go or who to tell.

He was famous. No one was going to believe me. All of this made me recall my initial reason for starting yoga – to heal. How far had I come from that initial aim? The weight of shame grew in me, and I started to cry everywhere I went. A female staff member told me to go for a walk to the other hotel and get a cup of tea. She thought I was upset that Dave and I were separated.

I told myself that I should never have trusted him, but I also did not know what to do to get out. This man, my guru, had total control of my life – my job and at the time, my housing and food. And he had told me that the longest journey I ever had to take was to my heart. My heart had led me to become a yoga teacher. Now I was in L.A., trapped. How did my karma yoga, my service to my teacher and his lineage, turn into this violation?

Where is Dave? I thought. Why isn't he here? I wanted him to save me. It felt like I was in a dream, and my dream took me back to when I was seven and had been betrayed by someone, and all of the other disappointments, betrayals and bullies in my life. How could this happen again with someone I trusted?

Two days passed. He was teaching that night, and I was supposed to help students out of the hot room if they fainted. I was in the corner on the far left, but I knew he could see me out of the corner of his eye.

During class, even though I was supposed to be the one helping others, I collapsed several times. He moved to me and exclaimed proudly, "See what I did to you. I make your practice beautiful. You have no idea."

Class continued, and he boasted about how handsome he felt. "I looked at myself in the mirror today, and I said to myself, 'You are looking good.'"

With every word that spilled out, I felt like I was being stepped on. Crushed.

Where am I? What world allows this to occur? I thought as I continued to move through the yoga poses he called out.

After class, I called Jesse, my love from Boulder, to try to tell him what was going on. "Jess, things are weird. I am having to rub his feet… and…" I didn't tell him that my guru had raped me.

After the training lecture later that day, I was told by staff to stay with our teacher. I did as I was told. My guru ordered me to find him a pillow. I brought him his tea. He acted like everything was normal. I cried a little bit and looked down at the floor while thinking, they invited me into their yoga family, and they use and treat me like I am a slave. Everything is really fucked up.

I brought him up to his room around 5:30 am after the Bollywood film. It was the same routine. He didn't say anything. I didn't say anything. We arrived at his door. He said, "Come in," and pulled me into his room.

Again, he proceeded to take off my clothes. I fought a little and then I surrendered. I disassociated from my body. I could very well not have had a body.

I said, "No," but he didn't listen. It was happening, again.

He was on top of me like a wild pig, grunting and sweating. It reminded me of the horrible experience I had in high school. I was horrified and collapsed under his weight. He kept going. I just wanted it to be over.

"This time I am going to ejaculate," he said.

He told me that he wanted me to cum. He rubbed me really hard, but I pushed his hand away. He told me to get on top of him. I did as I was told. And then I collapsed, but that didn't stop him. He got on top of me and ejaculated all over my stomach. It was over. I was numb.

He got up, went to the bathroom and returned with a towel. He threw it in my face.

I don't remember cleaning myself off. I don't remember getting dressed. I don't remember returning to my room. I felt like I had become less than human.

Later that night, it stung really badly when I peed. My belly was swollen and bloated. I had developed some kind of urinary tract infection. My body was really mad at me, at him, and at the whole world.

At a staff meeting the next day, I felt disoriented — voices were faint, and my eyes became foggy — and then I would come back to a clear focus. A staff member leaned into me and said, "Wow, you really took one for the team last night." I winced. Surely, she couldn't mean what I thought she meant.

Jamie, one of the staff members, saw that I was acting weird; she knew I was in pain and crying a lot. She pulled me aside and said, "Maggie, tonight I am going to stay with you and Boss."

"Ok, great," I said. "That would be nice."

We stayed up with him watching Bollywood movies, and then around 4am, we walked him up to his room. It was surreal. I was still in this strange daze, aware only of my bladder infection. I was not really thinking anymore.

He pointed to Jamie. "YOU this time," and then he turned around, expecting her to follow.

Jamie whispered to me, "Maggie, don't leave me."

I wasn't going to.

"Boss, I am going to stay with Jamie," I said. "We are just going to massage you to sleep, and then we are going to leave."

He didn't say anything. He ignored me. Jamie and I followed him into the dimly lit room. He undressed and put himself on the bed. We rubbed his back. After about fifteen minutes he started to snore. And we quietly left.

When Jamie and I arrived in another room, she looked at me, grabbed my arm and said, "Did he rape you?" I looked down and didn't say anything for a moment.

"My bladder really hurts," was all I could say.

"You know your body is angry about what happened," she said.

I hung my head, knowing my body was speaking the truth I couldn't bring to my lips.

The next day I called my mom and asked her to wire me some money to leave, but I didn't tell her why. Dana, a woman I knew from

51

L.A., picked me up and drove me two hours to Ojai, California. She was the first person I had seen from the outside world. We danced all weekend together.

"Dana, I have something to tell you," I said. "He forced himself on me. My yoga teacher. He forced himself on me. He said it was for my own good."

She listened and then shared a story about a shaman she lived with many years ago who would call her into his office to have sex with him.

"He called himself an alchemist," she said.

"Right, an 'alchemist'." I stared blankly.

I felt a deep sense of ease and fell asleep in the backseat of her car knowing that someone came to save me. And knowing that someone else knew my truth. We drove to the beach and shared a picnic. Together we watched the waves of the ocean. She leaned over to me and said, "It won't always be this way."

I looked at her. Her face was lit up by the golden rays of the sun. We walked back to her car, and she drove me to the train station. I was headed back to Eugene, Oregon. It was time to go home.

My boyfriend, Dave, was surprised to see me back home so soon. I didn't want to reveal my secret so I only told him, "The guru knows what he did to me." We didn't talk more about it. We got drunk and made love. He took me out on his motorcycle, and we cruised around town.

"I am going to go stay in the woods," I told him. "I just need some quiet time."

After a period of retreat, not knowing what to do, I found myself in Pittsburgh, teaching at a studio that had veered away from the scripted teaching. They followed the leadership of Mary, a senior teacher who had since distanced herself from the organization in L.A. Under Mary, I could still teach yoga, but I didn't have to say the words of the guru. I was still teaching the sequence, however, and I knew I would run into him eventually.

I got sick trying to do a juice fast and spent most of my time sleeping when I didn't have to teach. I taught football players and a movie star, which felt inspiring. Maybe there was something worth holding onto in my teaching career. I still felt loyalty to the lineage, and I searched for healing through the yoga practice while knowing first-hand exactly what the man behind it all was capable of doing.

So far from him and what he did, on the other side of the country, all I could remember was him as a caricature, with his pidgin English and his stupid jokes. I couldn't remember what I had thought was spiritual about it – it was an exercise sequence. Dave came out to see me. While our relationship had its ups and downs, the guru's betrayal had ripped me apart. It also ripped Dave and me apart.

During the month of my 28th birthday, I went wild in celebration of life. I got a massage by this woman who was a Mayan-trained healer for the womb, drank whiskey, and bought myself pretty things. I started a gratitude practice and wrote down lists of what I was grateful for. On January 30th, during a yoga class I was teaching in Pittsburgh, I felt a presence with me. It was a very maternal feeling. I felt scooped up in the arms of love, like I was being told that everything was going to be ok. A few days later I learned that my grandma Opal had passed peacefully in her sleep after ten years of battling Alzheimer's.

Grandma Opal was a big beacon of love in my life. She was a tough mountain woman who had lived through a lot. I looked up to her, especially as I was coming to terms with what had happened. Before her disease, she spent the last years of her life studying the genealogy of our family. She told me the story of a distant aunt who was raped on her farm as her family was being killed by Confederate soldiers at the end of the Civil War. My mom's family still owns this piece of property in Appalachia. A little more than three months after I was raped, I returned to this land to say goodbye to my grandma by placing her body in the ground at the family cemetery.

In less than a year, life had brought me a lot of tough lessons about betrayal, power, the shadow, sexuality and death. For the first time, I shared what my guru did to me with a special mentor, Michaela. She encouraged me to dance for my spiritual practice. I felt powerful dancing. The way I felt in my body changed when I danced. I could erupt like an earthquake. I could shake it all out – shake out the confusion, and the past. My breath would sink deep into my belly and something mystical would overcome me. Through my breath I could be the ocean, vast and powerful, more than a match for some twisted guru.

Nearly a year after the assault, I finally began to speak up to other people in my former guru's community and was stunned to find out I wasn't the only one he'd assaulted. I was also surprised that people continued to defend him. He had not just been my guru, he was a global personality with hundreds of studios across the world. And the system, without him, helped a lot of people.

My desire to further understand the betrayal of my yoga practice and body grew, and with encouragement, I went to New York City to study with Regena Thomashauer. At Regena's School of Womanly Arts. For the first time I didn't feel alone. The room was filled with four hundred women, many of whom shared similar experiences of sexual abuse and betrayal. With Regena's encouragement, the women were dealing with the trauma in a different way than I had ever seen; they were dancing in a wild display of divine radiance. They weren't letting it steal more from their lives – they celebrated themselves as sexual and powerful beings.

"When a girl knows herself, she won't be an easy target for a predator. That is what the pleasure revolution is about," she said.

I immediately knew in my body that through the pursuit of pleasure, I could stop the cycle of abuse that so often becomes a generational curse. Pleasure is a discipline. Pleasure is our birthright as women. How and with whom we share our pleasure is our power.

That evening, as I was taking a shower, I looked down at my body. My eyes traced down my belly button to my vulva. I patted the soft tuft of black hair. I began to softly caress myself as water droplets pooled on my breasts.

I closed my eyes to feel more.

I took a breath.

As I felt the water drip down my body, I recognized my body as sacred, and I felt a renewal, a baptism.

The next day, out of the blue, my former guru called me on the phone. It had been nearly a year since I'd last spoken to him. My hands shook as I took the call.

"Maggie… this is your guru," he spoke slowly.

"I need to talk to you about what happened. I was only trying to help you," he said. "I need you to forgive me. Do you forgive me?"

I had just had a powerful experience dancing in a room full of amazing women who saw the Goddess in themselves, and suddenly the twisted guru who raped me was asking me to forgive him. I was speechless.

"I swear on my children's lives," he kept repeating over and over. But he is not apologizing, I was thinking.

"If you say something, you will ruin the yoga community," he said.

I will ruin the yoga community, I thought. I didn't rape anyone.

I stayed quiet and then blurted out, "Forgiveness takes time. You can't just ask me to forgive. You hurt me."

He continued, "I thought I was helping you. I thought it was best for you. I am your guru."

"How could you think what you did was helping me?" I asked, stunned by his statement.

"I thought it was best for you," he said.

I started to cry, "*How* could you think what you did was helping me?"

I knew the real reason he called. A big lawsuit was coming out, and he was doing what he could to maintain his influence on the community.

I was not the only one. It had happened to other girls. I felt enraged that he had endangered my life, raped other women, and was spineless enough to try to avoid responsibility for what he did. A far cry from the master yoga teacher he pretended he was.

Asking me to forgive him was another stab in my gut. I was the one hurting. And yet, a part of me did want to forgive him because the anger felt so heavy. I was twenty-nine years old, and it was like a cage keeping me from who I wanted to be. Why wasn't he taking responsibility for hurting me and others? Why was he misusing his power? Why did he rape me?

I hung up the phone without forgiving him.

Now, four years later, I still do yoga, but I quit teaching the yoga sequence designed by my former guru. I've tried teaching other forms of yoga, but stepping on the mat is harder now because it forces me to remember what has changed and the pain I'm in the midst of transforming. I keep looking for a new practice and a new way of being with myself, and I just end up coming back to the practice of being in the present moment.

Under the direction of my former teacher, I spent years bending myself into shapes, and now it doesn't really mean anything to me anymore. All of the emphasis on an aesthetically compelling yoga poses seems shallow if it is not accompanied by some deeper inquiry into why we practice.

In Buddhism, there is the acknowledgement that suffering exists. That is the first Noble Truth. We suffer, injustice happens; scary and hurtful things that we did not plan occur. We come to realize, though, that there is a way out of suffering through what we call dharma. Our dharma is our life's work and offering. It can be reduced to all of the wisdom that we have accumulated and are then able to share in order to help others find freedom from their suffering.

It is the difference between living in a way that is full of self-interest vs. living in service to the benefit of all beings. When we live in service, we can walk courageously as Bodhisattvas, knowing that our suffering is never in vain.

As a child I watched my dad bow a thousand times a day. A bow is essentially a prostration. It is the reverent acknowledgement of the Bodhisattvas who have walked before us. It is because of everyone who has walked before us that we can now take up the practice of being present with our lives and others.

A vital role of the teacher is to remind the student that practice is not a self-centered pursuit. Good practice reminds us of our interconnection with all of life. In becoming a student we choose to trust our teacher in order to receive their teachings. During the process of learning deep truths about our selves and our abilities, we also have to be able to trust that the container will be held for us to continue diving into the psyche and beyond. As a student we are not surrendering our safety and agency to another and should not be asked or forced to. For a teacher to misuse their power during a student's realization of interconnection and oneness is a monstrous action that deserves to be exposed.

While my own journey has been full of setbacks, I remember that any journey we may be on is mysterious. I used to think I was singled out because I was weak. I know, however, that I am neither weak nor naive. I was singled out because I was there. I wish that my willingness to serve and the kindness I was offering had been met with mutual respect.

When I close my eyes and feel deep into my body, I find an ecstasy in knowing that I belong to myself and the cosmos, and something returns. I can feel more deeply, surrender my pain, and waves of breath wash over me like the ocean. And somehow, despite it all — I am free.

About the Author
Maggie Marie Genthner

What did you want to be when you were eight years old?

A country music star.

If you could give one piece of advice to your younger self about your orgasm, what would it be?

Know your body by practicing self-pleasure so that you can show someone with your heart and breath how to splay you open to the Goddess.

If your orgasm had a voice, what would your orgasm say to you about the piece you wrote for this book?

Your heart is ready to soar.

FIVE

"I have a gift for naming the obvious — for speaking to the elephant in the room. Clearly this can be annoying for some and liberating for others. I don't mind — I believe clarity is necessary for evolution."

—Cyd Saunders

MY VAGINA SAVED MY LIFE
by Cyd Saunders

I always thought that listening to one's genitals was limited to annoying hippies and even more annoying New Age people, or that your name had to be Dakini something-or-other to have a talking vagina.

Apparently not.

When I first heard her speak to me I was shocked – it was undeniably my vagina talking to me, clear as day. One would imagine that the first time you hear you vagina speak would be a sacred, spiritual experience, that she would be heralding great news of profound significance – the Great Womb has spoken, and so on. My vagina in a rather ordinary but firm way told me on no uncertain terms to stop sticking things in her.

At first I was amazed and excited about this interaction. Surely it was a sign of my maturity that I was "listening to my body".

After the excitement, however, I started to feel really annoyed. Her message was perplexing. How could I possibly live a life putting nothing in my vagina? I love sex, I love exploring…. What did it all mean? My vagina was bossing me around.

I became rebellious, like a naughty schoolgirl, fighting the wisdom of my own vagina. Maybe she won't notice if I continue to put things in her, and who is she to tell me what to do? How bad can it be? Maybe I made up that vagina voice, and it was not even true. I did not want my vagina to wreck my life!

I continued to have sex, but something horrible kept happening. No matter how slow and beautiful my lovemaking was, within twelve hours she felt sore, scratchy and raw. I thought I was having a candida crisis, so

61

I put myself on a super clean detox for four months. It was to no avail – I still had the same symptoms. I had never experienced anything like this. I was an orgasmic woman, and sex was easy for me, or so I thought.

I continued to fight the wisdom I had received. Maybe if I use more lube, go slower, only have sex when I feel like it – everything, anything but to stop having sex.

This experience was not happening on its lonesome, no way. At the same time as my vagina spoke, I was also in a spiritual emergency. My 12-year marriage was over. It was a huge relief, but I was smashed into a million pieces. My shit had hit my fan big time. It was time for an overhaul whether I liked it or not.

My socialized being was breaking apart; I could no longer continue to be who I was before. My boat was setting sail for new waters, and I knew I had to be on it. There was no room for anything inauthentic – all my old stuff, my socialized self, was being questioned, and I had to move quickly, because there was no way I was going to miss such a magnificent opportunity to sail into a brave new world.

I had a lot of time to think on the boat. After twelve years of mothering, I was no longer a 7/24 mum; the boys were with their father half of the time. That was a big lifestyle change, and I had time and space to unravel.

My talking vagina moment was the grand opening of my embodiment.

Embodying was a super painful path at first. Once I started to feel things, all the emotions that I had managed to keep a lid on surfaced with a bang! I was full of stuff – trauma, pain, grief, anger, terror – all the things that I couldn't handle before and that were not complementary with my socialized self came spilling out of me. It was hugely painful, like being stabbed with a million spears. I had a problem staying dedicated to composure and control when I was shaking with trauma or being wracked by terror.

My life had not been out of the ordinary. In fact, I think I had been quite fortunate. I had, however, had a life with all the knocks and hurts that all humans experience. I live in a society that is driven by success and money, with little or no room to honor the truth of being human. A society unwilling to slow down and take the time to allow people to be themselves. Look good, get a job, find the perfect partner, get behind that white picket fence, have perfect children and live together happily for the rest of your lives. Excuse me while I have a small vomit in my mouth… Some people fit beautifully into this ideal, but in my humble experience most do not, and I hurt myself trying to be what I thought I "should" be.

I realized during this powerful time that I had built a lot of my socialized self on sexual objectification, which I had experienced strongly as I blossomed into puberty, thanks to the men in my family. (I had some creepy uncles!)

There is great power in sexual objectification. In my late 20s, I realized that people wanted to have sex with me. (I just thought they were being nice to me before that!) I could have sex with whomever I wanted. In my 30s, I became an orgasm expert. I was super sexy and could turn it on with a bat of an eyelash. All of this seemed to work for me – I felt special, and I was validated time and time again from the world outside of myself. I had no idea that I was sexually objectifying myself. It had been projected on me at such a young age, I knew nothing different.

I related to everything and everyone in sexual terms. In fact, I think I had bouts of sexual Tourette's syndrome, if there is such a thing. I began to notice that I was ever so quickly able to give everything a sexual bent. For many years I had no filters – it shocked, delighted, liberated and offended people. It got me the attention I thought I needed.

It was an overwhelming force in me and yet a limited expression of who I truly was. It was beyond my awareness until my vagina spoke to me. That was a major reality check; in fact, it was a huge relief, shocking at first, but with time I have slowly started my release from the world of sexual objectification.

I have decided to let my vagina be the boss of me. I have stopped "sticking things in her", and as I allow her the space to detox, recalibrate, breathe and rest, my whole person has also begun to detox. I find myself in a very, very creative space. For the first time in my adult life I have no partner and am not having sex. I have indeed begun a very intimate relationship with myself. I am getting to know myself; I take myself for big walks on the beach. We spend a lot of time in my art studio. I love being in nature with myself, and I rest a lot… I have a sneaking suspicion that this could be my best relationship ever.

As I've been listening to my vagina, I have been delightfully overawed by a cascade of revelatory awareness. I feel like I am waking from my slumber. My life is becoming a truly peaceful, new world. I am choosing to walk the path of powerful beauty.

About the Author
Cyd Saunders

www.cydsaunders.bc

What did you want to be when you were eight years old?

When I was eight, I fantasized about being a secretary. My father was an accountant, and he would bring me home stationary, stamps, staples, pens, paper, receipt books... I loved all that stuff. I would busy myself writing receipts and stamping everything, including my own school books; there were red ticks and blue stamps everywhere. I felt so grown up. I am still obsessed about pens now.

If you could give one piece of advice to your younger self about your orgasm, what would it be?

Forget it! Choose your sexual partners well, based on kindness. Relax and breathe – your orgasm is a gift to be received, not something to achieve. Mindful masturbation is not what you do as a substitute for not getting laid. Mindful masturbation is what you do to forge the road home – to you. Knowing how to connect with yourself well means knowing how to connect with others well. Who doesn't want that?"

If your orgasm had a voice, what would your orgasm say to you about the piece you wrote for this book?

My orgasm would smile beautifully at me and say well done. The sex educator in me would add, the correct physiological term for a woman's genital area is vulvo-vaginal, but it was just a bit too wordy for my story, so I simplified with vagina.

Anything else?

I would like to thank Dr Gregg Lahood, my Transpersonal Psychologist for traversing my spiritual emergency with me with such love, care, tenderness and respect, and for seeing so much more in me than I saw in myself.

SIX

"And the day came when the risk to remain tight in a bud was more painful than the risk it took to blossom."

—Anaïs Nin

THE SCRIPT
by K. Ronan

I found my orgasm on a snowy day in New York City. I was lying down in a meditative practice in which my clitoris was being stroked by a complete stranger for 15 minutes. Just another Saturday afternoon. I remember looking up and out of a window as tears rolled down my face. It was as though something was unlocked, released, a layer was peeled back, a whole under-world within me was exposed, a veil lifted. I found her, my birthright, my true heartbeat, my orgasm. And then I gave her away.

Let me start by saying I use the word orgasm a little bit differently than is common in our culture. Unlike climax, that ecstatic peak in sex or self-stimulation in which the body releases oxytocin and endorphins, orgasm to me is more of a current. It is a subtle flow of energy, a life force that is always there and can be harnessed any time. It is a gateway to being more present and to feeling more in the body. And that is what I was seeking when I went to meet that man, even though I could not put it into words then. I was embarking on an unintentional journey to feel more.

At the time, I was a woman who had tied everything up into pretty boxes and bows. My books were lined up handsomely on a beautiful bookcase in a lovely New York apartment in a picturesque neighborhood, paid for by a job that looked really good on paper. My nails were the perfect shade of OPI dusty pink, my highlights a sun-kissed blonde. I was yoga toned and pretty and smart and slowly dying inside. I had not had sex in two years. My life revolved around my career, and I simply avoided the messiness of intimacy with men. I put energy towards controlling what was seemingly controllable in life and avoided what was not. But there was an ache inside that was growing, that could not be denied, a desire to come alive that was welling. I could sense there was a deeper level of feeling, something that wanted to be expressed that was stifled. I also had a sense that if there was an access point to that level of feeling, it could likely be the part of my body that had the highest concentration of nerve endings. Always one to find the most expeditious path towards a goal, I went straight for the clitoris.

I now know that I am a woman who lives in the width and not just the length of life, and so it is no surprise that my research in feeling did not stop on that snowy day. The 15-minute practice turned to sex, the intimacy grew, and I fell in love with the man who had witnessed my tears that day. And then… I got hooked. The "shutter the windows, turn off the phone because I am not coming out anytime soon" kind of hooked. Our sex was intense, highly pleasurable, and deeply awakening. I was discovering parts of myself that I did not know existed. Before, I'd felt like my sexual energy was a round sphere, smooth and symmetrical. I was discovering a shape more like a crystal, with hidden crevices and facets that captured light and darkness in a far more complex manner. I wanted to go deeper to discover more. My orgasm, and thus my feeling body, took on a whole new dimension. I was bright and vibrant and buzzing. There was a current running through me. The discovery of how much I could feel, of how deep the access, was life-changing. It wasn't that I had not been feeling – I simply hadn't known my *capacity* for feeling.

As little girls, we inherently know our bodies are meant to move, to dance, to cry, to giggle. We know how to feel without thinking. We are unapologetic about expression, until one day we get a fateful message that we need to temper that expression. It comes in the form of a whisper at first (dear, don't dance like that; it is not appropriate) and then the roar of criticism gets louder (you are a slut, a bitch, too loud, too much, too demanding, too too too). We begin to learn how to make ourselves wrong from a very early age. Layers slowly start to build up under cultural scripts that are handed to us. We step into prescribed roles; that of friend, daughter, wife, mother, lawyer, fill in the blank. We adopt those identities and cling to them for dear life. It gets harder and harder to feel under the layers of identity, even if we have chosen them. They can become like numbing agents wrapped in the cloak of what it means to be an "acceptable" woman in society. It is as though those identities take on the feelings that are assigned to them, and our innate knowing and feeling body takes a back seat. And the more we say no to our own primal expression, the more we subscribe to a culture's preconceived role of who we should be, and the less we feel.

I started to strip away the layers of identity, the roles that seemed far too limiting a definition of me as a woman. I found an access point to feeling more via the practice and via sex. And then the access point subtly started to shift. Instead of it being my life source, I was slowly but surely giving the honors to him. He became the access point, the agent. That well-composed woman was becoming like a crack whore. I wanted his love, his attention, and his sex. I saw that as my gateway to feeling. I wanted my fix, and so I handed my orgasm over to him.

My lover was young, on a deep spiritual and sexual quest. He had other lovers, even lived with one of them. I felt the pain of abandonment whenever he would leave and return to her, each time another little piece of my heart breaking. I would stuff down and silence the voice of self-love that said this does not feel good so that I could have more. I assumed the role of victim. I settled, I didn't speak up, I resorted to tears when anger was the real emotion; I acquiesced time and time again. I stopped speaking my desires. I lost weight; stomaching all the pain and anger had taken my appetite. It was masochistic, really. I had never lost control like that. I actually had a friend beg me on the street to stop making myself sick over this man. *Why would I stop when I could have another ounce of his love*, I thought? I had come undone. I did not care about nail colors, or board meetings, or the latest hot restaurant in New York. I did not care if the dry cleaning had been picked up or if I got eight hours of sleep. I didn't care about anything but when I would get another hit. I had never lost myself like that — not to a man, not to anything. I was unrecognizable to myself.

Sometimes we have to go to the dark place, to the shadow of ourselves, in order to truly surrender. I think that is especially true for someone like me who created a semblance of safety by trying to control all I could. And yet, I think I wanted to lose control for once in my life.

Control is an illusion, after all. I had found a portal to a deep pain that needed healing. If I was the victim, it was of my own choosing. I could feel the darkness inside. I could feel the trauma, the abandonment, the jealousy, the shame and the feeling of not enough. Oh, the not enough. There was the gripping, the absolute need for this man to fill a hole in me that felt bottomless. I followed my shadows, knowingly, willingly. I got to know them intimately. It was actually an intoxicating recipe for self-discovery.

Addiction has a long line in my family; I come by it honestly. Because I could happily stop at two glasses of wine and (mostly) left the recreational drugs behind after college, I believed I was "free" of addiction. Thank goodness that gene skipped me, I always thought. The funny thing about tapping into your orgasm and feeling more is you learn a lot about what binds you. If orgasm is a current, moving like a steady mountain stream, our deep-seated fears are like the boulders revealed, impeding the flow. It is said you cannot selectively feel. So when I opened up my orgasm, I opened all of my feeling body, including the shadow parts of me that I didn't think were pretty enough or appropriate enough for my script. Perfection smacks of endlessness, they say. I could feel my addiction for this man and how I thought his love could fill the parts of me that I myself did not love. What had been stuffed and repressed finally got to see the light of day. It was not pretty by conventional standards, and yet it was breathtaking. I was in a state of painful yet liberating awe. I had no idea my life force had so much depth and so much breadth. My shadows were calling out to me, they wanted my love. I was learning that those dark parts of myself deserved all the love and attention that the light ones did.

The cycle of heartache continued for many, many rounds until there was nothing left for me to give to the cycle or to the relationship. I was physically, emotionally, and energetically spent. There was literally nothing left; my body was limp. The orgasm that I had cultivated when the relationship started had all been spent. My unique currency had been depleted, my account was empty, and it was clear the bank was not him. That bright vibrant buzzing, that current, were all gone. I knew enough to know I wanted them back.

I started a long process of self love that will last a lifetime. I got to the real work of what it means to be alive via a slow death. I got reacquainted with the internal voice that knows, and I followed her. I used the pain of my hook to that man to access my own love, and I found tremendous power there. I immersed myself deeply into me, uncovering layer after layer of self with curiosity and humility. There was no more script. I was making a new one. I began to get reacquainted with my orgasm. I began to know and say what I wanted again. I could see that playing victim was far easier than owning what I wanted, although far more costly. I could see I was hardly a victim at all; I had actually called the entire experience in as the creator that I am. I think there was a part of me that wanted to die so that I could be reborn. I wanted to unravel the life I knew, I wanted to be unbound. There is sweet, sweet power and liberation when we step into owning the fact that we have created all of it.

And in this new location, I can see that my orgasm is light and dark. She is at once measured and completely out of control. She can reveal total surrender when, and if, I surrender to her. She is a gateway and a home. She is my muse. She is freedom, and she is discovery. I listen to her, so very carefully now. She has more facets than ever before, and I know I will never abandon her again. I know now that no man can "give" her to me, she is mine. We are creating a life, she and I, and it is far beyond the limiting beliefs of what I thought possible. On the other side of losing my orgasm, I rediscovered it and the woman I am. She is fucking fascinating. I would not have known her had I not come undone. Thank goddess for coming undone is what I say.

We are told as women not to lose ourselves, but don't we do it all the time? And don't we call it all in, the drama and pain and resurrection? Isn't there power in knowing we conjure all of it for our own unfolding? What if we actually celebrated it as part of the creation of a new life, and what if there were so many lives to live within this one? What happens when we shine a light on the shadow so that our full essence can be revealed?

Don't we have to lose ourselves to find ourselves? Don't we ache to strip down the layers of pretense, of the rather shitty bill of goods we have been sold about what it means to be a woman? I for one will say that the crumble, the disarray, the messy, was such a welcome sigh of relief. Because after destruction there is life, there is awakening, there is rediscovery, and there is rebirth.

As women we have a delicate responsibility for our orgasm, for the energy it produces, for how we cultivate it, harness it, and for how we spend it. It is a valuable currency, and we often barter it unknowingly. To the jobs that are slowly killing our souls, to the culture that says our bodies need to look a certain way, to the relationships that have run their courses but that we stay in anyway. We give our life source away. And then we find it anew. A wise woman once told me, never abandon yourself again. I would like to add to that, make sure to abandon yourself at least once so that you can find your way back to the woman you were meant to be.

Find the thing that has cut off your orgasm and go there. Go into the deep, dark crevices of that which scares you and get real uncomfortable. Let us support each other's coming undone. I honor your addictions, your shame, your fear, and your not-enough. I applaud it, because I can see the woman who is rising on the other side. The key is in knowing that this is part of your creation. We birth and rebirth. We know the cycle of life in our bones. I want women to know they can embody that cycle. They can lose themselves and find themselves again. In fact, they must. We did not come here to play small. My wish for women is that they can feel more, all of it, the light and the dark.

I want for women to throw away their scripts. There is no script. You are the script.

About the Author
K. Ronan

What did you want to be when you were eight years old?

A teacher

If you could give one piece of advice to your younger self about your orgasm, what would it be?

Trust yourself, trust your body, trust that inner voice inside yourself – she is your guide, and she will never steer you wrong.

If your orgasm had a voice, what would your orgasm say to you about the piece you wrote for this book?

Thank you. This is the true expression of me, and I hope that other women can connect to our story and feel into their own orgasm.

SEVEN

"There is a basket of fresh bread on your head, yet you go door to door asking for crusts."

—Rumi

SISTER
by Anna Perry

A nun passes by
No more nun than I,
Sister, we've more in common than meets the eye.
Your vow of chastity not unlike mine,
only married to two different ghosts.

About the Author
Anna Perry

What did you want to be when you were eight years old?

When I was 8 years old I wanted to be a performer on Broadway, a marine biologist and a singer.

If you could give one piece of advice to your younger self about your orgasm, what would it be?

Orgasm is one of the great gifts of being human. It belongs to you. Be healthy, be kind, and above all, LOVE yourself.

If your orgasm had a voice, what would your orgasm say to you about the piece you wrote for this book?

Orgasm is compassion, pleasure and joy. It's available to you whether the person you are in relationship with participates or not.

EIGHT

"It is not the end of the physical body that should worry us. Rather, our concern must be to live while we're alive — to release our inner selves from the spiritual death that comes with living behind a facade designed to conform to external definitions of who and what we are."

—Elisabeth Kubler-Ross

Big O Hidden in the Middle of the Alphabet
by Fig Ally

I've always found it amusing that we call it the "Big O" when o is tucked away in the center of the alphabet, just like a precious clitoris you have to search for in order to reap its rewards.

I've known my entire life that I am a lesbian, announcing at the age of four at the family dinner table, "When I grow up, I'm not going to marry a man. I'm going to marry a woman." My parents and siblings were unfazed and disinterested; my mother responded, "That's nice, dear – now pass the mashed potatoes."

In each grade during grammar school, I regularly asked girls to marry me, and just as regularly my mother received phone calls from concerned mothers about their frightened or confused daughters whom I'd inadvertently traumatized. It became a familiar routine – once a week or so, the phone would ring at about 5pm, and when my mother answered, the conversation went like this: "Yes, Mrs. Hill (or Mrs. fill-in-the-blank for the latest girl I'd proposed to), I understand. I'm so sorry. Yes, I'll speak to her. Thank you for calling." I'd eagerly run to my mother's side as she called out for me, hoping the call was news that somebody's mother had approved of the impending marriage, but alas, the story was always, "Honey, that was Mrs. Hill (or whomever), calling about her daughter who is afraid because you asked her to marry you, and, well, though I love you very much, honey, you have got to stop asking girls to marry you, because it confuses them, and sometimes it scares them."

My unvarying question – But why, mom? – was always met with, "Just don't, honey."

You'd have thought I was on track to be quite the romancer given my early bravado, but by high school I had grown silent around girls and young women. I still fell in love often, but now I was silent about it, keeping my longing to marry each one a secret as I watched the flock of newly-budding heterosexual boy-girl interactions around me. I watched the girls on whom I had crushes blush and grow unnaturally stupid and clumsy around boys that didn't smell nearly as good as I nor provide the girls with any of the poetry I had inside me.

In high school, I redirected my energies into the drama club and the school newspaper. I couldn't articulate it at the time, but it was a choice I made from a place that had become frozen inside me – not from constant rejection or reprimand, entirely – but instead from a fearful place. If I were happy, I'd betray my family's legacy of female misery and suffering that romantic relationships inevitably led to. When I was five years old, there was a night when we all sat down at the dinner table – my mom, my dad, my two brothers and I – but there was one person missing, my fifteen year-old sister. I asked why she wasn't at dinner. My inquiry was met with stern looks from my parents, and silence… no explanation. Later that night, as I went to bed in the bedroom I shared with my sister, I inquired again where she was, because she still wasn't home, and I was met again with a stern look and silence. The next morning, I woke up early, hoping to see my sister in her bed, only to find she still hadn't returned home. Once more I asked and was ignored. I was to find out she had gotten pregnant, and my father made the decision to eject her from the house and from the family, with no input from me or my brothers, or even my mother. My sister had shamed him, and so she was banished – to where, I wasn't sure. All I knew was that the sister I loved had suddenly disappeared without warning, and it had something to do with her being in a relationship.

Months later my mother would sit me down and tell me that my sister had gotten pregnant, and that it was the way things went for women who became pregnant at early ages — their lives were forever ruined, and they brought shame on themselves and their families. I reminded my mother as she gave me that talk that I wasn't going to marry a man, that I was going to marry a woman, and that I didn't think I'd be pregnant. My mother sighed and told me to stay away from relationships and become the nun she thought I was on track to become.

My sister never returned home. I looked for her daily when I awoke. I cried myself to sleep nightly, worrying about her whereabouts. Where was she staying, sleeping? Who was feeding her? Did she cry for me the same way I cried for her? Many years later, I learned how horrible it had truly been for her when she suddenly lost her family and home. The guilt was a constant with me — why was I, a small child, unable to save my only sister from suffering and hardship? Why was her life so different than mine, simply because she had gotten into a romantic relationship?

I didn't realize it at the time, but I had become frozen in regard to any romantic notions — even with a girl — because of course, I feared banishment from my home, from the family, even from myself. Isn't that what happened to the women in my family when they became romantically entangled? They became strangers even to themselves.

I went through high school without so much as the kiss of another girl — no dates, no mushy love notes, though I had so many written in my heart. My mother and father were happy that I seemed to be a nonsexual being on track to be single for life. After high school, I went on to college, but I still lived at home, as I was paying my own way, and I couldn't afford both rent and tuition. All throughout college, I remained frozen romantically... silently falling in love with many young women but never acting on it. Since I gave off a librarian nun energy, seemingly uninterested in anything as mundane as romance, no one ever approached me, either. Still I remained unconscious of the why, telling myself I was just protecting myself. I was too busy working and going to college to have time for romance.

Once I was through with college, I got a job and moved into my own apartment. I thought to myself, now is a good time to play catch-up and ask all the pretty women out. I still feared that romance would be the end of me and the beginning of a vague misery, but I was bolstered by the fact that at least I couldn't get kicked out of my own apartment for having romantic relations. I had a friend, Larry, who had a roommate, Katie. She had an edge to her, smelled of men's cologne and made it known that she liked me. One evening I showed up at Larry's house to go out with him and Katie answered the door. She said that Larry unexpectedly had to work late, but I was welcome to come in and sit with her for a while until he came home. As we sat on the couch, I was very aware of my physical attraction to her and hers to me. We talked, and she suddenly leaned in and kissed me for what seemed like a wonderfully long time. One thing led to another, and she took me to her bedroom. She removed my clothes, asking me if she could tie me to her radiator. Now this may seem odd, but I wasn't experienced in any way; I was just so happy that somebody was interested in having sex with me that I quickly agreed. I was eager to see what bit of frolic awaited me, but once she had me tied to the radiator, she, still fully clothed, left the room and then the apartment. I called after her, "Hello! Hello, are you coming back? Where are you going?" Katie never came back. I remained naked and tied to the radiator that thankfully never turned on (just like me) until Larry came home, mortified to find his friend in such a state.

Undaunted, I figured Katie was just a minor stumbling block on my way to what I surely anticipated as my romantic highway of love. A few months after Katie, I met another woman at a gym I frequented. I worked up my nerve and asked her out, and that led to several successful dates. Those then led to intimacy —well, an attempt at intimacy, for I became so overcome with emotion that I threw up (I had enough sense to turn my head and miss her) and began crying uncontrollably. Needless to say, she politely asked me to leave after I'd cleaned up.

Upon reflection, my pattern of avoidance was still present. Either I picked someone who wasn't available, or I physically worked myself up into such a stressed state that when it came right down to the moment of actually having sex, I threw up around the poor woman. I was still protecting myself from becoming ruined, though at the time I called it, "ehhh, just strange luck".

I went on to meet another woman, and this time we managed to have sex without me being tied to a radiator and abandoned, or me throwing up and bursting into tears, but I couldn't feel a thing as she touched me, kissed me, whispered of her attraction to me. I didn't understand why I felt nothing, and I wanted to tell her that I couldn't, but I was afraid of insulting her, so I lay there like a mummy. (As if she wouldn't notice that.) She asked me what was wrong – had she offended me? Instead of telling her (and consequently myself) the truth, I lied, telling her I was just tired. We continued dating and having sex, but I never really felt a thing whenever she touched me. I always faked it to "protect" her, having a very present fear in my head that this was going to be what got me expelled from myself forever, from my family forever. I knew it was a terrible way to go about my intimate life, but I didn't yet have the presence of self to change it; I feared that process would be even worse than the numbness I felt during sex. I was afraid I'd disappear, just as my sister did all those many years ago, and that I'd never be found nor find myself again. Eventually, that relationship ended, and I was free to shroud myself in as much myth, fear and denial as I wanted.

I remained single for a few years after that, once again comfortable in my avoidance until the day my dental receptionist introduced me to her best friend, and I fell in love quickly. She was, without hesitation, free and uninhibited. Like me, she came from a tough childhood and had the emotional scars to prove it. Her old pain often interfered with our intimacy, and that made it possible for me to remain numb in our sexual encounters, even though I truly loved her. I longed to tell her but was afraid to say it out loud; I was afraid that she'd see me as defective and then abandon me. We remained together for many years, madly in love – I was never fully present with her sexually, but I loved her just the same. I never knew how much I was cheating her and myself, because I was steeped in my fear and wounds. And although she loved me, she didn't have enough emotional fortitude to press me on it.

After many years together, I came home one day to find her dead by her own hand, her childhood scars having gotten the better of her. I lost my love and any chance I might have had to be fully present with her on any level. Shortly after her death, as part of my grief and healing, I decided that I was going to risk being fully present sexually with myself and another, if ever that opportunity should come again. I undertook a journey to the center of my alphabet – slow, difficult and painful, but I was determined to not die too as she had done. I would begin living truly, without fear of losing myself.

I had lost myself already, so in truth, I could only find myself again.

About the Author
Fig Ally

What did you want to be when you were eight years old?

At age 8 I wanted to be three things all combined: a spiritual teacher, radio show host, and writer.

If your orgasm had a voice, what would your orgasm say to you about the piece you wrote for this book?

Thank you. I love you. Welcome home.

NINE

"Ah, women. They make the highs higher and the lows more frequent."

—Friedrich Nietzsche

YOU'RE WEIRD
by Bob Pattee

September, 1976 – Boston, Massachusetts

Julie: When I met Bob, he was a freshman, and I was a sophomore.
He was older than me. He had taken some time off before college. He
was tall, thin but not scrawny, and kind of cute. He had a sexy gap
between his front teeth. We worked together a couple days a week in the
pub in the Student Union. We both had work-study jobs there. He was a
busboy, and I was a short order cook. I broke the ice with him one day by
commenting that we both had that gap between our teeth, and that some
people think that's really sexy. We spoke a few more times, and he seemed
smart and funny, not snotty and pretentious like a lot of the wealthier kids
at Boston University. He was kind of shy, but he seemed pretty smart. I
figured I might have a shot with him, so whenever we were on the same
shift, I'd strike up a conversation. As soon as I could, I turned the
conversation to sex. I think I started with, "So, how many people have
you had sex with?" or maybe, "So how old were you when you first had
sex?" I told him my story: I first had sex when I was 13, on a camping trip
with my parents and some friends of theirs, with an older guy who was a
friend of my parents. Bob didn't think that was very cool, but I explained
to him that I had kind of initiated the whole thing. I told him I thought it
was a good goal to have had sex with as many people as you are years old.
I was 20 and a little bit ahead of the game, having had 22 partners. Bob
was way behind, having had only 7 or 8 partners. I was hoping I could
help him catch up.

Bob: I met Julie when we both worked in the Student Union, first
semester of my freshman year. She was friendly and funny and had the

93

kind of body I like: thin but not scrawny, almost-but-not-quite flat chested. She could have been taller – she was maybe 5' 5" or 5' 6", but as Kate said about her later, she had a body that wouldn't quit. Of course, Kate probably added "except for the tits," but I liked her tits. She was obviously smart, and obviously not one of the entitled rich kids from New York or the Middle East. Those kids didn't have to do work-study jobs. She wasn't what I'd call pretty, but she was very smart and engaging and fun to talk to and had a sexy gap between her front teeth. I didn't know that was supposed to be sexy until she told me, but when I thought about it, I had been attracted to other women with gaps. When I thought more about it, I remembered that my mom used to have a gap like that until she got her full dentures and had them made pearly white and without the gap. My father didn't like that she had the gap removed. Neither did I. When my dad got his dentures, he insisted that the dentures be made exactly the same tobacco-stained yellow as his natural teeth, and with the same crooked and uneven teeth. Julie liked to talk about sex, which I thought was pretty cool. Pretty soon I got the idea that I could have sex with her if I wanted to. I wasn't sure, though. She had a good personality, and she was fun to talk to and had that cool body, but she just wasn't that pretty. I always thought I should be with a prettier girl, like Suzie, the stripper.

Julie: After I had told him the story about how I lost my virginity, I asked him to tell me about how he lost his. He told me the story, but the only detail I remember was that she wouldn't let him come because they didn't have a condom, so the next day he got a condom and called her up to see if they could get together again. They did that night, and he tried to get her to have sex with him again, but she begged off because she said she was "too sore". He thought maybe that was just an excuse. I thought maybe he had a nice big dick. I explained to him that if he had a big cock, that she might really have been too sore. He seemed a little embarrassed and said that other girls he'd been with had told him that it was kind of big. I got more interested.

Bob: When I told her about losing my virginity to Liz on the bench seat of the Fairlane, and how Liz made that excuse the next night about being too sore, she explained to me that it might not have been an excuse, especially if I had kind of a big cock. Hmm, I thought… maybe it is big. That'd be cool. It always seemed kind of normal-sized to me, but I guess I hadn't seen that many cocks, especially not hard ones. Suzie said it was, but I always figured she was just saying that to make me feel good. Liz said it was big when she was playing with it before we fucked that first time, and it's true that it was almost as big around as her wrist, but she was such a tiny girl. But maybe …

Anyway, around this time I met Jennifer, and after knowing her for a couple weeks, we went out to the Eliot Tavern with her friend, Lisa. Lisa went to the bar at one point and came back with a weird, long-haired dude who claimed to be the son of a certain celebrity chef. He came over and sat with us and eventually said he had some coke we could all do if we had a place to go. So we all went to Jennifer's apartment in Brookline and did coke, and that turned out to be the first night I fucked Jennifer. Which was a really sexy night – almost as sexy as the first time I fucked Julie, not quite two months later. And I guess the fact that Jennifer said it was the first time in a couple of years that she came while being fucked was more confirmation that maybe my dick was big – maybe I had even gotten pretty good at this sex stuff. I guess maybe reading all those books about it was paying off. Julie and I continued to be friends, and we still saw each other a couple of times a week when we worked in the pub, but for the moment, I was really enjoying being with Jennifer. That time when she and I took my nieces to the Halloween parade was really fun, and it made me start thinking maybe I could marry her. She drove that green Cutlass with the drop-top, and one time we were going someplace, and Phil – the Karate Kid – was with us. It was warm for October, so she had the top down, and Phil jumped over the door into the back seat. I tried to do the same thing and ended up banging my knee on the top of the door as I tried to swing over. Really cool move, dude.

Julie: Somebody else, some yuppie girl from the Midwest, got to Bob before I could, but I didn't let that stop me. I saw my chance around Christmas break. Events conspired – yuppie girl had gone back home for the long break, and my roommate and I were staying in town – we were moving to a different off-campus apartment. I asked Bob if maybe he could help me move my stuff, since he had a car, and he agreed. I had already moved some stuff and had just a few boxes of books and some clothes and stuff. Bob brought a six-pack for us to share. We got my stuff moved and then sat in my room in the new apartment and talked and smoked cigarettes and drank a couple of beers, but he didn't make a move on me. Weird. Finally, he said he guessed he should get going, and I realized I was going to have to make the move.

Bob: So things were going pretty well with Jennifer, but Julie still seemed interested – and interesting – and the more I got to know her, the more I liked her. Jennifer was great, and sex with her was just amazing, but I never really felt like we were best friends. Julie seemed like somebody I could be best friends with AND we could fuck. She was just really smart – way smarter than Jennifer – and really fun to talk to. She did have that annoying conversational habit of always finding some way to put herself down – usually, but not always, something about her looks – and always in a half-joking way, but other than that, she was a lot of fun. Then Jennifer went away for a few weeks – I guess it must have been over the long Christmas break.

Jennifer was away, and Julie and her roommate were staying in town for the break. Their families couldn't afford to fly them home, especially Julie, who was from Bermuda. And they had gotten a better off-campus apartment for second semester and were moving over the break, and Julie asked me if I could help her move some heavy stuff, since I had a car. I guess the apartments were furnished, so they just had their belongings, and they had walked some stuff over, but Julie still had boxes of books and stuff. So I said sure. I thought maybe this was when I could make my move on her – I think she was thinking the same – if only I knew how to make a move. So we moved her stuff, then we drank some of the beer I'd brought and talked, and smoked cigarettes. And I tried to figure out, when's the right moment to kiss her? Or do something – I don't know, put my hand on her leg or something. I think I was waiting for that perfect romantic moment like in the movies, when the stars and the moon align, and the romantic music swells, and eyes meet as lips purse and heads move, hesitatingly, closer and closer. But it just never came, and finally I just wussed out. I got up to go. Wishing I could just fucking man up. It was like Leslie from high school all over again, only this time I was not only not a virgin, I was pretty fucking experienced. But still. So, regretfully, I got up to go.

Julie: I didn't know what else to do, so I said, "You're weird."

"What do you mean?"

"Any other guy would have made a move on me in this situation."

"Well, I wanted to, but . . . I guess I'm kind of a romantic, and I was waiting for the right moment or something, I don't know. I'm kind of shy."

"Let's have those last two beers."

"OK."

So he sat back down, and we opened our beers, and we kissed, and it was good; he was a pretty good kisser.

Bob: Thank God for Julie. She told me I was weird, and when I asked why, she said that any other guy would have made a move on her in this situation. I mumbled something about being a romantic and wanting the moment to be right, or some crap like that. I'm not really sure how the conversation went after that, but anyway, before long we were sitting on her bed, kissing. Then we were lying down. The kissing was really good, we were both good kissers, not clumsy at all, gentle lip and tongue play alternating with deeper thrusting, just enough spit to keep things very slippery, occasionally more forceful kisses with teeth bumping against each other, then sometimes moving to ear and neck kisses and back to lips, as we warmed to the mutual moment. Our hands, at first tentatively touching and caressing each other on the arms, moved to touch the skin of one another's faces and necks, then each to the other's ass, ribcage, then back to neck and face, as the kissing grew more passionate and we shifted our bodies to press against one another.

By now I was pretty hard, and I made sure she could feel me through my jeans as I pressed my hard cock into her pelvis, and we rearranged our legs so that I was pressing against her pussy, and our breathing and our heartbeats quickened. I moved a hand to one of her small breasts, first just a thumb on her nipple, then my palm, caressing the nipple in a circular motion, then gently kneading her now erect nipple with thumb and forefinger, still outside her shirt. Then I moved down to her waist and put my hand inside her shirt, on the skin between her belly button and the button of her jeans, starting to move up toward her breast, and she pulled away and took off her shirt in one motion, so I took off mine and started kissing and licking her small, firm, pink nipples. God, she had a beautiful torso – small, firm breasts with pink, erect nipples, about the circumference of a nickel coin, smooth, white skin – and I continued to lick her nipples and I got a thigh between her legs and started to press it rhythmically between her legs, sometimes coming up to nuzzle and kiss her lips and neck and ears some more while doing her nipples with my hands, and at some point she put her hand on my jeans, rubbing my cock through the denim fabric. Then we moved so that she was on top of me, and she was kissing me hungrily, first on the mouth and face, then moving down to my chest, her hands reaching down to unbutton my jeans and unzip my fly as her mouth – her tongue! –moved down to my stomach.

She pulled my jeans down, and then off, and took a moment to comment on my sexy black underwear, the nylon briefs that Suzie, the stripper, had bought for me not much more than a year earlier, then she removed those and started kissing and licking my hard cock. At first she was too gentle, I could barely feel it, but she knew what she was about, and soon she had the whole length of it slippery with her spit and was taking it, not the whole thing, but about the top third of it, the head and the really sensitive part just below the head, into her wet, slippery mouth, moving up and down on it with her mouth and tongue. She had one hand on my cock to help guide it, at least some of the time, but at some point she must have been using her other hand to take off her own pants and underwear. Sometimes I clenched my Kegel muscles, which makes my cock swell even bigger and increases the sensation, and when I did that, she would slow down and back off a little bit, so I think she thought I was on the verge of coming when I did that, but I was nowhere near coming just then, I was just trying to get more sensation, and God it was feeling so great, nobody had ever sucked my cock so well before. I was grabbing onto the bed covers with one hand and sometimes caressing her apple-scented hair with the other hand, and reveling in the sex and the sensation and this incredibly hot, sexy, smart, thin but not scrawny girl going down on me. And after a few of my clenches she must have thought I was really about to come, either that or she really was ready to get fucked, because all of a sudden she moved up over me and without even using her hands at all, slid her wet pussy right onto my hard cock in a single move, and now I was deep inside her tight pussy, not too tight, we were a perfect fit, and she was moving on me and kissing me and I had my right thumb on her left nipple, my fingers on the side of her ribcage, and we were kissing and thrusting, and she was making little moaning sounds of pleasure and our teeth sometimes bumped together the way they do when the kissing is really going well, and she was wet and I was hard and we were both thrusting in time with each other, and then I planted my elbows and grasped her hips and lifted her a little bit off of me so that I could hold her still and I could really start thrusting myself into her hard and fast and rhythmically, pounding into her sweet wetness and continuing to kiss her as her breath quickened even more and I could feel her tightening herself on me to get the most sensation, and I squeezed, too, to make myself that little bit bigger, but not so hard that the sensation would overwhelm me and I would come, just enough to give her a little more, and then she was gasping and moaning and, oh God she was coming, clenching me rhythmically and taking deep quick gasping moaning breaths as the waves of pleasure washed through her, and after a bit we slowed down and I lowered her down a little bit and continued to fuck and kiss her, now more slowly, more gently, and we kissed more slowly and deeply, but gradually after she caught her breath, I lifted her again and moved faster and I could smell her sweet juices and I moved faster and deeper into her and I could tell she was getting close again and I was getting there too and I wanted to hold on for her so that she could come again, and I could hear her getting closer, feel her tightening herself on me, feel her getting closer and I was getting closer, almost there, and I just had to hold back for a few more seconds, a few more, almost, and I kissed her deeply, intensely, our tongues together pushing and intensifying the full body sensation for both of us and yes, yes, she was going over the edge and I waited to make sure and yes, there, right there, she was gasping and clenching me again and oh, God, I let myself relax and oh, oh, I was thrusting and coming and God the sensation on my dick and my whole body, the electricity and the sudden wetness inside her making her even more slippery and I was coming, but still hard for a little longer, and I kept thrusting and we kept kissing and moving and I let her down onto me and for a minute or two we just held each other, our bodies sweaty against one another as we caught our breath and felt our hearts pounding one against the other and I started to soften and we laughed and kissed a little more and I thumbed her nipple again and she shivered at that, and then, after another minute or so, as if to prove a point, she lifted her head and looked me in the eye and clenched herself again, tighter this time, and pushed me right out of her.

After that we kissed a little more, and then, having had so much pleasure from her mouth at the beginning, I moved her up so she was on her knees, straddling my face, and with my hands on her breasts and on her ass, I started licking her pussy, still wet with my own juices, and licking her lips and her clit with my tongue and my lips, hungrily, wetly, rhythmically, sometimes more slowly and sometimes faster, just the tip of my tongue and then my whole mouth, tongue, lips, finally planting my face into her and settling into a steady rhythm with my tongue until she began to gasp and buck against me one more time. Holding her ass with one hand and thumbing a nipple with the other, maybe slipping my finger into her mouth for a moment, and oh, yes, again, again, third time's the charm, and as her body twitched with the aftershocks and she lay down on me and kissed me again, deeply and wetly, mingling both our juices with our spit, reveling in our mutual pleasure, hands softly roaming each other's body in the afterglow, she told me I was pretty altruistic and I had to ask her what that meant.

Postscript:

Jennifer arrived back in town the following night, and I spent the night at her place and fucked wildly, but I don't remember any details. Two women in 24 hours! A few weeks later, just before the second semester started, I left my job at the pub and got my hack license and started driving a cab. Julie suggested a "rematch", and I declined. Jennifer broke up with me, and I was heartbroken, at least for a month or so. For months afterward, if a woman walked by wearing the same perfume as Jennifer, I would become partially erect. Later in the semester, still reeling from the breakup with Jennifer, I asked Julie out to dinner – we went to an Italian place in Porter Square that's now a stationer – and afterwards, she invited me up. I came up to her apartment, but her roommate was there, and the walls were pretty thin, so I made some excuse and went home. A few years after that, during the spring of my senior year, Julie and I went to a bar early one Friday afternoon and drank beer and shot pool all afternoon. We finally went back to her place and tried to fuck, but I had had way too much to drink and had my first experience with an uncooperative erection. We did manage a little bit of penetration, I think, but maybe not. And a week later she suggested a "rematch" and I declined. What the hell was I thinking?

That one night at the end of Christmas break, freshman year, would become my go-to jerk-off fantasy for years.

About the Author
Bob Pattee

What did you want to be when you were eight years old?

A scientist, observing Halley's Comet from a nearby space station in 1986.

TEN

"We can make our minds so like still water that beings gather about us that they may see, it may be, their own images, and so live for a moment with a clearer, perhaps even with a fiercer life because of our quiet."

—W.B. Yeats

MY TRUE GARDEN
by Susan Motheral, PhD

I moved back to Texas in the early 1980s and during the next twelve years, I had seven boyfriends. I dreamed that I might create a life with each guy, move to a new home and maybe even start a family. For a few years, I had been ready for a different house with a bigger garden, but I kept putting off buying a new place, and instead I said yes to one new boyfriend after another.

After Fred and I split up in 1993, I decided to get a new house before I got a new boyfriend. When I elected to take a break from new boyfriends, I also gave up on the idea of having a baby. At 41, I was utterly ambivalent about having a child and heartbroken about letting go of the dream. And then I found The One.

I fell in love with the 1950's green tile in the master bathroom, the unfinished oak floors beneath the green shag carpet, and the half-acre lot, with the beautiful old trees in the front yard and the neglected back yard. I could already imagine the Oriental and brightly colored Moroccan carpets I had collected for years providing the perfect covering for the hardwood floors. In the living room, there was space for a piano, and in the back yard, there was space for a big, covered back porch – the perfect place for enjoying fiery North Texas rainstorms. I could already see the garden filled with rosemary and lavender and antique roses, and ponds with a waterfall where the frogs could hang out in the summer. The sounds of falling water and the croaking frogs would serenade me and lull me to sleep.

On Halloween 1994, I said "I do." I bought the 1955 vintage ranch style house. The property was located in an older neighborhood I had known and loved since my childhood, with sidewalks and wide, tree-lined streets. The house and garden were full of potential, but when I purchased the property, it was decidedly ugly, as in UG-LEE. Essentially, nothing had been done to it since it was built. The windows were those aluminum ones so popular in the mid-1950's. The air and heating systems were kaput. The so-called living and dining areas were really dead rooms, cut off from the rest of the house. The kitchen/dining/den area was a wonderful 43 feet long, but only 13 feet wide. It was like a bowling alley, way too narrow for the home of someone like me, who wanted flow in my living space and room enough for parties. There was almost nothing worth keeping in the back yard – twenty six volunteer trees, a magnolia tree in an awful location, dead grass, and a falling-down greenhouse. It all had to go.

I spent the next year designing the home I wanted to inhabit, both indoors and out. I poured through home magazines, searching for ideas and accumulating stacks of clippings of things I liked. My dream was of a beautiful place with warmth. I love to cook, and I envisioned a kitchen big enough for more than one person to work, with barstools for friends to sit on and visit while I cooked, views of the gardens from every room, a place of comfort and elegance. The plan was big and bold and included things like moving interior doors, and expanding the kitchen/den area to the back of the house, with a new fireplace inside and a big back porch outside.

Demolition began on a snowy day in January of 1996. As the house was being dismantled, I barely noticed that I had gained forty pounds in the two years since starting the project. I had put all my energy into creating my home while ignoring myself.

Once the work on the house was underway and spring was beckoning, I shifted my attention to designing the garden. In July, the house was far enough along to start work in the backyard. Step one was to terrace the property and improve the fertility of the soil. The subsoil at my home is called caliche, a calcium carbonate material that forms a sort of natural cement. As part of the terracing, we took out truckloads of caliche and replaced it with fertile soil.

By mid- August, as the new kitchen cabinets were being installed, and walls were being painted, I went for my annual wellness exam. As I told her about my renovation project, the doctor urged me to slow down and reduce my stress. And then she found a lump in my right breast. A mammogram the next day showed that the tumor was growing out in one direction. Within three days, the diagnosis of malignant breast cancer was confirmed.

It was incomprehensible to me that I should have cancer. Not me. Not now. After I left the doctor's office, my mind was topsy-turvy with a host of uncertainties and fears. All I could see was the possibility of death. I tried calling a couple of close friends, but there was no answer. Trying to figure out what to do with myself, I chanced upon an estate sale and went in. Now I had something else to focus on, and I did find one thing that I needed that day – a fireplace grate, still in use in my den.

What followed were tests and retests, and a trip to the Dr. Susan Love Breast Clinic at UCLA for a second opinion. In mid-September, I painted the smallest room in the house in brilliant teal and turquoise colors that remind me of the Mediterranean. I took this time of creating something beautiful in my home to make decisions about my treatment. After two surgeries, I began a clinical trial to test a new chemotherapy regimen. Within two weeks of starting the chemo, I was bald, and my hormonal system was shot. I wore a blond wig or a brightly colored scarf and kept my anti-nausea pills in my pocket. Since I had opted for a lumpectomy to remove the tumor and spare the breast, radiation treatments were planned for the spring. Maybe by then there would be something blooming in the garden.

It was clear to me that I had to find a better way to live.

I joined a cancer support group. An Australian couple, Dr. Sam Ford (a theologian) and his wife, Jane, led my group. The focus was on doing what we could to help our bodies heal, based on findings from the relatively new field called psychoneuroimmunology. Sam absolutely loved saying this word. His face would light up and he would draw out the saying of it, as if it were the magical elixir that would cure everything.

Cancer does not discriminate – by gender, age or race – and out of cancer, a community of loving support came into being, bringing together a group of people I would have never met otherwise. Each week, we would talk about our experiences, sharing our struggles and meditating to clear our minds. One week, at the end of our meeting, six women who had had breast cancer surgeries of various sorts went into a private room and bared our chests to share our scars. The six of us covered the range of surgical options, from my relatively minor lumpectomy to women who had double mastectomies, one with and one without reconstruction. My scars, which loomed large in my mind, were relatively minor. I found a deep level of gratitude for the choice I made to keep my breast. Over time, I could see for myself that those who kept sight of their joy lived best, even if they did not survive their cancer.

When a long-time friend told me I would have to wait to move into my new home until I was finished with chemo, I put my hand on my hip and said, "I don't think so." The house was finished enough to be habitable, and the garden reconstruction could carry on with me living in the house. So, in November of 1996, three days before my third chemo treatment, I moved in.

Family and friends came to help. My realtor (the mother of my new sister-in-law) and my mother's housekeeper packed the kitchen, my mother's best friend cleaned out the pantry, and my brother took a day off to do whatever needed to be done – pack/organize/supervise. Together, we made it happen. The evening of the move, my close family and I made a toast in my new home, drinking red wine out of my grandmother's crystal wine glasses.

My life was moving along, yet one of my first thoughts every morning was that I had cancer. I felt betrayed by my body, and I struggled to find joy. Anger and sadness do not provide fertile ground for hope and joy.

Prior to the cancer diagnosis, my plan had been to resume dating in the fall of 1996. Now, when I considered the possibility of a new relationship, I could not imagine telling a new man that I had been diagnosed with cancer, that I did not know if it was going to return, and that there was no way to test for it. So I did not let any new men into my life. Men from my past would call, and I just ignored them. There was only so much talk or even awareness of cancer that I wanted to share.

This included Hank. He had been my lover on and off for about eight years. Between my boyfriends and his girlfriends, we were together. Our friendship was an easy one. Every now and again, we would spend an evening together, cooking dinner, laughing and talking of life and art. And we played, with no expectations other than that we would have fun together and be friends.

In December, Hank asked me to spend an evening with him, and it was clear to me that that my thoughts and feelings about our sweet friendship had changed, and my sensual responsiveness had disappeared. My body had been so faithful to me through my life – from my early explorations as a girl who was fascinated with her body, to the curiosity of exploration I had experienced with my lovers – and now I felt nothing. As I was making choices for life, my ongoing fears and worries left me feeling that I had little to share. Instead of welcoming Hank, I sent him away, ending our close connection. In the aftermath of this, my juice for living dried up even further. I was withering on the proverbial vine, physically, emotionally, spiritually, instigated by my deep despair, which only magnified the impact of the hormonal changes in my body.

Over time, my home – and especially my garden – became my life raft. Outside of work, I put almost all my energy first into creating them and then into maintaining them. In the midst of radiation treatments in the spring of 1997, my doctor asked me a loaded question: "How are you, Susan?" I burst out sobbing, reciting the litany of what was wrong in my life. She suggested we put me on an anti-depressant for a year.

That spring my hair started coming back. It had been almost straight before chemo, and now was growing in kinky, curly and baby-fine. My garden was rich with the smell of humus from the compost I'd added. I was overseeing the construction of new ponds on the south end and a new garden shed on the north. I picked a sunny, out-of-the-way place on the newly terraced upper level of the backyard and planted yellow pear and sweet 100 tomatoes, and spinach. When the ponds were complete, and the waterfall was flowing, I added goldfish purchased at a bait shop and soon the first frogs showed up, calling for mates to join them in the pond and serenading me with their songs of summer.

That summer, I spent a week at Ting-Sha Institute, a cancer camp, in beautiful Point Reyes, California with other cancer survivors, where we did things like paint and dance and play, beginning to see that we could live beyond our worries and sadness about cancer. I was surprised when a painting flowed out of me. I carefully rolled it up to take home. It represented hope.

A month later when I returned to Dr. T for my well-woman check-up, she found a mass on my right ovary. The surgery was scheduled on the same day I'd had my lumpectomy the year before. Now I had three surgeons and additional disruption to my hormonal system.

I continued to work in my garden and to beautify my home, and, for a long time, I veered in and out of a spiritual and physical wasteland. My garden was blossoming as my own skin was drying out. Within two years, I was diagnosed with vaginal atrophy. I finally realized my spirit and my body – all of me – demanded the same reclamation and nurturing that I had been giving my home and garden.

It did not happen quickly, but I was persistent. I kept exploring, just as I had when renovating my house and garden, except this time my project was me, and the research was centered on what would bring me back to life. I remembered what it felt like to feel good in my body, so I started researching my orgasm, something I had turned away from for ten years. When I felt myself beginning to truly relax so that orgasmic energy could flow within me, it felt like the opening of a door in me that had been nailed, bolted and barricaded shut. I was not sure this door could or would ever open again. This opening paved the way for an expanded sense of joy in my life that shows itself most clearly by the fact that I look younger and more radiant in photos than I did ten years ago.

I began to see that my body is a temple, that it is sacred, that it is not separate from 'me' and that all of me deserves respect and kindness and love (as does every other being on the planet). I also saw that I flourish when I am bathed in these sweet blessings. And I began to understand that my body is the vessel through which the love in me comes through into the world, and that my life force is resilient. I discovered that just like my garden, my body blooms when it is well tended.

Now it is eighteen years after my diagnosis. I no longer think of myself as a cancer "survivor". I am alive, and once upon a time, I was diagnosed with cancer. For about sixteen of these years, I have spoken with the occasional cancer patient who finds me. Ironically, while I was writing this, one of my colleagues was diagnosed with locally advanced kidney cancer. My conversation with him reminded me how much I love to talk to people diagnosed with cancer, especially soon after their diagnosis when they are often a bit baffled, see death looming (whether it is true or not), and have lots of decisions to make. I know that some live and some don't, and that what I know now can help others bypass some of the stuff that was so very challenging for me. Along the way over these eighteen years, I had a teacher, Martin, who was told at 35 that he would die in a few months; he did die, but it was 37 years later.

Who knows why some live and some don't? Martin believed that it had to do with consciousness and the chakras. I am not sure. What I do know is this: In a mind that is settled down, the love that is the essence of who we are shines through, and that love is the ground of ultimate healing. It is always in you and me just waiting for us to glimpse it, and sometimes we can't see even a tiny sliver of it. It may or may not keep us alive in the presence of cancer. Nonetheless, there is grace in seeing that a sliver of light can open the universe to a person, as if just the taste of it is enough for this life.

When I painted my painting at Ting-Sha in Point Reyes the year I was diagnosed with cancer, I had no idea of the depth to which it would speak to me. I framed it and now it hangs in my home. What I see in the composition is something like seaweed that keeps its integrity and expresses its resilience as it responds to the ebb and flow of currents of life. The predominant colors are green and violet. This green is the color of the heart chakra, which represents compassion and the bridge between the physical and spiritual worlds, while the violet of the crown chakra represents my connection to God, the infinite consciousness of all that is. The painting I created seventeen years ago laid out the parameters of the path for me to find a better way to live, and stands as the perfect expression of the resilience of my human heart with its expanding access to compassion and the blossoming of my connection to spirit.

My home and garden have become my sanctuary, rather than my life raft. I love living in the beauty of what I have created. Others seem to enjoy sharing it with me. It is both elegant and comfortable.

The garden has its own cycles. It goes dormant for a couple of months in the middle of winter, and the flowers start blooming in February, typically beginning with fragrant white narcissus. Next come yellow forsythia and daffodils and thrift, a hot pink spring phlox. The white flowers of the Mexican Plum tree and the pink flowers of a Saucer Magnolia follow. Then, by mid-April, the garden erupts with roses. The waterfall flows all year, even in the ice and snow.

The goldfish have mated in the ponds over the years, so the current fish are descendants of those purchased at a bait store so many years ago. Over the years in the garden, I have seen so many critters wandering about my yard – lizards and snakes, raccoons, possums, armadillos, red and grey foxes, and even an occasional great heron, stopping by to check out the fish in the pond. In the late spring, several species of dragonflies come in for the warm months and by June, they are joined by frogs and toads, who create a serenade all summer as they call each other to mate in the pond. There are butterflies all summer long, and in late September, the monarchs stop by for a few weeks on their way to Mexico for the winter. Many of the roses bloom again in the fall. Occasionally, my favorite rose, *Souvenir de la Malmaison*, is blooming still at Christmas.

My true garden is a place of remarkable fertility and it is right here, right now. The life force is vibrant and resilient in me and in my garden. Almost twenty years after deciding to take a break from dating, I have started dating again. I wrote this story because I want every person on the planet to know that just because you can't feel your own life force right now does not mean that it is lost and gone forever. It is hiding out, waiting for you, too, to let your mind settle so that you wake up and smell the roses.

About the Author
Susan Motheral, PhD

www.drmothcral.com

What did you want to be when you were eight years old?

When I was eight, I was a tomboy, and it was clear to me that I would become a football player when I grew up. My six-year-old brother and I each received a football uniform from my parents that year for Christmas. We had a big, open back yard then. Mike and I would suit up and have great fun playing a two-person version of the game, throwing the ball, kicking it around, and tackling each other and rolling on the ground. This was long before I thought I would become a lawyer or found my love of psychology. What a hoot!

If you could give one piece of advice to your younger self about your orgasm, what would it be?

Have a love affair with your body. Slow down and enjoy each drop of sensation – all sorts of sensations, from the taste of a ripe summer peach to things like stubbing your toe. All of this is a divine gift, a sacred manifestation of the life of a spiritual being having a human experience.

If your orgasm had a voice, what would your orgasm say to you about the piece you wrote for this book?

I am so glad that you now see this story more clearly and that you shared it with the world. It's important for people to know that humans are resilient, that our capacity for pleasure was in us when we were born and will be with us until we die. We just forget sometimes.

ELEVEN

"I have spent most of my life unlearning things that were proved not to be true."

—R. Buckminster Fuller

FINDING MY WAY
by August Mohr

When I first read Betsy Blankenbaker's announcement that she was collecting stories for _Autobiographies of Our Orgasms,_ I was excited about contributing. My partner and I had just completed a two-day workshop about communication, personal power and personal boundaries, and I had concluded the workshop by working on an internal confrontation with my late father. I had practiced telling him "No!" with power and strength.

I was feeling free, grounded, and empowered. I was excited at the prospect of writing about my own personal journey in reclaiming myself and my own personal boundaries. I thought I would examine how my father's abuse was a violation of my personal boundaries as a child (to put it very abstractly). I had recently been seeing how my own boundaries being violated had influenced my later tendency to push at the personal boundaries of women I was attracted to, how I had difficulty asking for what I wanted and made others uncomfortable with my manipulations, and how my compliant and people-pleasing nature was giving nothing of my real self. I told myself that I was ready to jump in and tackle my previous misconceptions about how seduction works; I wanted to examine the subtle kinds of boundary-violating pressure that I had learned to apply.

But that particular topic never really caught fire. It was too new an insight; it was still too much in my head and not in my heart.

I thought for a while that I might write about the lack of sex throughout most of the 25 years with my late wife and how we had begun to heal from that. I could discuss what I now think about the root causes of those problems and our contributions to them. My wife's barely-

117

glimpsed memories of possibly having been the subject of pedophilic bondage photography by the neighborhood "creepy guy" at age five were certainly a factor. So was her mother's suicide attempt in front of her when she was a young teen. And there was a lot more, all of which challenged her sense of safety. My late wife's various ways of attempting to cope and heal from that, to maintain control, clashed intensely with my insistence that I could not ask for what I wanted, that everything had to happen "spontaneously". Both of us digging in our heels about what we "dared not say" resulted in downward spirals that left us at one point not having sex at all for over two years.

But no matter how I framed the story in my mind, I kept coming back to the simple fact that I have not yet dealt with those issues deeply enough to focus on them, especially publicly. I still have self-pity, guilt, and anger, all too intertwined to be able to share that story coherently. Besides, a lot of it is her story, and she's no longer here to tell it.

I thought about writing about significant turning points in my sexual history, things I had learned and the people from whom I'd learned them. In the spring of my freshman year of college, I connected with a girl who had been becoming a friend. We were both virgins. It took nearly three weeks for her to get a prescription for the Pill and for it to take effect so that she would be "safe". It was like three weeks of extended foreplay; we knew where we were going, we knew we were going to get there, and we knew we were not going to be able to go there right now, so we learned some patience in our passion.

But it's all too easy to pretend that the "things I had learned" were all that it was ever about. It's too easy to gloss over the profound difference between knowledge in my head and the fears and criticisms embedded in my sense of my own being.

I also thought that I might write about my relationship to pornography throughout my lifetime. That's certainly a subject that I suspect most men wrestle with in one way or another, and which I also suspect most women really don't understand from a man's perspective. I have read numerous articles on the subject that mostly seem to confirm the authors' biases. It's extremely rare to find someone reporting research on the subject in which the results are surprising to the researcher.

More importantly, I have yet to find any research that distinguishes between different content types in pornography, other than "soft" or "hard", despite the fact that subtle differences can be tremendously important to men – and I'm not talking about fetishes. For instance, when I was a teenager, there was a "huge" difference between Playboy and Penthouse: you could count on there being some photos in Penthouse that showed a hint of labia minora, where Playboy "tastefully" never did. To a teenage boy, that could make the difference between getting off or not.

But when you come right down to it, all of those subjects are about the past. Of course, that is part of the concept of an autobiography. But while all these topics are things that I am still working on, I'm really more interested in exploring the directions in which I am growing, rather than the wounds that I am healing.

Right now I seem to be focusing on self-acceptance, on patience with myself and on truly being present to my experience. My partner is helping tremendously with that. We got together, in part, because we both value introspection, self-honesty, and awareness of our unconscious (as contradictory as that may sound). With her help over the past two years, I have been learning to let go of being goal-oriented in a sexual encounter and instead to pay attention to how I am enjoying the immediate moment, enjoying my sensations, enjoying my connection with her, enjoying my awareness of her sensations.

My partner has been helping me to radically change my relationship to masturbation. For most of my life I have felt embarrassed and even ashamed about masturbating. Oh, I can state boldly, "Of course there's nothing wrong with masturbating!" But I don't live that way inside. As a teenager, I hid any evidence that I might even think of such a thing, even though my mother conscientiously gave me books like Esquire's What Every Young Man Should Know. As a young adult, I never talked with my girlfriends about it, not even with my male friends, except jokingly.

The subject of masturbation was extremely charged between my late wife and me. When she found my stash of printed porn and my dirty towel, she was terribly hurt. "How could you leave that where I could find it when you won't even touch me?" I responded by getting defensive, claiming that when I tried to touch her, she pushed me away. She counterclaimed that I was not turned on when I tried to touch her, so there was nothing for her to respond to. We went through that same fight at least three times.

Things are truly different with my partner now, in ways that I had barely let myself imagine. Despite her own painful childhood and turbulent relationship history, she has been developing and integrating "sex positive" attitudes. And she has been responding with those attitudes when I go into my embarrassment and shame.

She has been experiencing some health issues, and right now she is far more interested in my giving her an hour-long massage than she is in fucking. She has been encouraging me to recognize that, as a man, in this particular body, I have a physiological need to "get off" more frequently than she does, in her particular body, at this particular time. She has been encouraging me to "take care of myself" – to masturbate.

I started out completely unable to tell her that masturbation was what I wanted to do. The thought of saying, "I'll sleep better if I get off, so I'm going into the other room for a little while. Is that okay with you?" was too painful to even imagine. The times when she offered to "do me," sitting next to me on the bed where she could comfortably reach my cock, lube and towels handy, her attention focused on me and my pleasure, I could reach an exciting peak that I then fell back from, but I could not ejaculate in front of her.

She wonderfully, lovingly accepted that this was simply where I happened to be at that moment. There was no judgment, no sympathy with my "problem", no "we'll fix this" determination. The question was merely, if this was not what I wanted, then what was it going to take for me to get what I want?

She repeatedly resists judging me while pushing me to accept what happens to be so, right now. That helps me transform the stuff I know in

120

my head into feelings in my body. I'm taking things I have known and could talk about, and I'm experiencing them as my new reality. We have discovered that when I am restless in the middle of the night, snuggling close helps. It helps even more when she calmly, quietly, affectionately takes my cock in her hand. I usually get hard immediately. If she does not attempt to arouse and stimulate me but rather stays calm, and if I allow myself to simply enjoy the pleasure of the touch and connection, my experience moves from my head into my heart and into my body, and I relax. I fall back asleep within minutes.

My body has been drinking in that profound acceptance. It nourishes me; it heals me. It helps me to treat myself with acceptance, which in turn helps me to treat her in the same way.

I have been learning to come in her presence, with her participation or not, with deep eye contact or not, touching her or not, smelling her or not, looking at her genitals or not. For the first time in my life, I feel I have a lover who wants me as I am. Of course with my previous lovers, it had been at least as much my problem as theirs, but here and now, at this point in my growth, I'm with a woman who supports my growth. I no longer worry about whether or not I meet her fantasy. She wants me to do better, to be better, but not by any external measures. She wants me to be better at being myself. And I'm discovering that I can sometimes actually be happy.

My original thought was to write about was how my father's abuse of me as a child had impacted both my ability to set my own personal boundaries as well as my ability to recognize and respect those of other people. That was my wound. I decided not to go there yet again. Letting that go seems to have allowed me to get deeper in touch with something in my life that is actually helping to heal that wound. Feeling emotionally safe inside myself is helping me to live with awareness and respect for others' emotional safety.

Having the power to say no from my heart and belly, I can say yes with something other than my head. When I can truly say no, I can accept that another person may say no to me. This gives me the freedom to ask for what I want and to be able to take no for an answer. I like that.

121

I've had another recent insight in how I relate to my partner about the effect of where my attention is. For most of my life, when I've had sex with a woman, I've been goal-oriented. In essence, I've been asking of her, asking of the space between us, what can I do that I want to do that will be OK with you? As a result, I was focused on getting what I wanted, not on her enjoyment. If you think about the dynamics of that, the result was inevitable: I was constantly crossing her boundaries, making her uncomfortable enough that her discomfort got through my preoccupation with myself and got me to change what I'm doing. Most of the time she had to speak up and say something – "that hurts" or "I told you not to go there". That definitely spoiled the mood.

Recently, by spending lots of time massaging my partner with an explicit "this is not seduction" rule, I've been learning how to be truly in the moment with her experience, enjoying her pleasure. When I am paying attention to how my touch is affecting her, even when it's erotic, I notice immediately when I get too close to something she's uncomfortable with, and I change what I'm doing before she needs to say something about it to me. That has allowed me to give her erotic pleasure that is not goal-oriented, that supports and nurtures her boundaries rather than coping with them or trying to get past them. I'm helping her to be in the moment, helping her to enjoy her body. And that does the same thing for me.

Thanks for listening.

About the Author
August Mohr

What did you want to be when you were eight years old?

I don't remember being eight very well at all. It was a pretty traumatic time in my family. My younger brother had suffered brain damage due to suffocation less than a year before, and he was not yet old enough to be moved into a state institution. He needed massive amounts of care with no expectation that he would improve. The family was constantly stressed, our parents were constantly fighting. I do remember emulating my brother's physical therapist; I helped with stretching his limbs daily so his muscles would not lock up. I felt like I was really making a difference. At eight I might have said I wanted to be an astronaut, but John Glenn and Yuri Gagarin hadn't flown yet. I might have said that I wanted to be a teacher, but I hadn't encountered any male teachers yet. I did play school with my sisters and other kids in the neighborhood, and I was always the teacher because I was the oldest. I suspect that, if asked, I would have said that I wanted to be a scientist.

If you could give one piece of advice to your younger self about your orgasm, what would it be?

Be kind, be gentle. It's how your body was made to work. Be patient, there's no hurry. It's meant to feel good, so enjoy the process as much as the end. And take your time coming back down, too.

If your orgasm had a voice, what would your orgasm say to you about the piece you wrote for this book?

Thank you for acknowledging me, for paying attention and not presuming that I'm exactly like everyone else.

TWELVE

"To orgasm is to flow with the essence of life."

—Wendy G. Young

FREEDOM:
THE STORY OF MY O
by Wendy G. Young

I'm sitting on the floor in the corner next to the big, white dresser.
I'm hiding. I play with my feet. They tickle when I touch them with my
fingers. "Ah. Hahaha. Hehe." I put my hands up high in the air and I
move them up and down fast! I'm excited!! I touch my feet with my
hands. This is fun! I curl my nose and open my mouth wide and laugh!
"Hahahaha." And then I remember the spot on my body. Touching it
makes me really happy. I put my hand there and smile. It tickles me. And
I laugh.

Suddenly, I hear a loud and scary voice say "No, don't do that."

I'm picked up off the floor. I stop laughing. The voice says I'm a
bad girl. I cry and feel tears on my face. The voice says if I do that again,
I'll die. I can hardly breathe as I scream and taste my tears.

The next time I let myself feel that tickle, that joy and freedom in my
body, was many years later when I was in college. My boyfriend came to
my dorm room on a Friday night to stay with me. I was in bed sick, so he
sat at my desk and did his homework. I felt comforted having him there
and looking after me. After a while he started kissing me. I enjoyed it. I
felt safe. He eased his hand inside my panties and gently rubbed his finger
on my clit. I had no idea what he was doing. I liked the sensation I was
feeling yet felt ashamed to tell him, like something was wrong.

Then suddenly my body jumped, almost like it was scared. It resisted
feeling the good sensation – the same one I felt as a young child. He
stopped immediately and asked "Are you okay?"

"Yes I am," I said, but that wasn't the truth. I was embarrassed and ashamed because I was completely disconnected from my sensuality. It scared me to feel pleasure.

For the next thirty years, I buried the joy and innocence I experienced in my body as a child. To feel safe, I mostly chose work over fun and solitude over socializing. I chose to build and sell a successful business over creating intimacy with a man, or with myself. When my business sold, I should have been celebrating the successful career I'd created, but instead I knew something was missing.

My friend Sheila Kamara Hay, founder of the Ecstatic Birth movement, suggested I invest in a sensual session.

"A sensual session? What is that?!" I asked.

Sheila explained that the session would be with Steve and Vera Bodansky, who have devoted their lives to the study of sensuality and orgasm. They've written several books and also offer private sessions for women or couples who want to study with them. As she spoke, I realized I had one of their books, *Extended Massive Orgasm*, but I hadn't taken the time to read it yet.

"The Bodanskys will teach you things you did not know about your own orgasm," Sheila said. "You will learn a lot about yourself, too."

Her words made me want to feel safe in my body again. I wanted to feel that tickle, that joy. I wanted to remember that my body was mine to enjoy.

"What is an extended massive orgasm?" I asked, now very curious on what my body was missing out on. "A full body orgasm that goes on and on?"

"Yeah. Something like that," said Sheila as she winked at me.

"People do private sessions? Really?" I asked. "I'll have to think about that. I would be way too embarrassed. I don't see myself doing anything like that."

"Just give it some thought," Sheila said. "I can totally see you doing this and believe you would benefit tremendously."

"Would I take off my clothes?"

"You get to decide how deeply you want your exploration to go," said Sheila. "Now that you know about it just let it settle in your body and let your intuition be your guide. If you are meant to have the session, you will."

I pondered the idea of a sensual session with the Bodanskys as much as I considered the idea of shopping for bras – which I avoided. I nearly dismissed the sensual session completely, like their book that I had left unread. And then, like Sheila said, I finally listened to my intuition instead of my judgment and contacted Steve to make an appointment. He said they were fully booked. I was so disappointed. A few days later, he contacted me again to offer a session after they had a cancellation. My body said yes, and so did I, even though my mind was thinking other thoughts: If any of my friends or my family knew what I was planning to do, they would ostracize me. How could I do a sensual session with two people I did not know at all?

It was a beautiful day in May of 2008 when I arrived for my session with the Bodanskys. I lived in Houston, and they were giving the sessions in New York City. I took some of the proceeds from the sale of my business to pay for the plane ticket and the sensual session. It seemed like an indulgence, but I decided to give it to myself as a gift for the painful journey I'd experienced during life. At one point, my therapist had told me I was depressed, but something in me felt there was more to it. Walking up to the brownstone that day in New York City for my session was the first time in my life I'd felt a sense of freedom. It was the first time I chose me instead of being concerned about what others thought.

I met Steve first and was offered a short, silky robe to wear. As I took the robe I thought, this is short and possibly one size too small. And then I smiled and remembered, what did it really matter?

After I changed into the robe, I was invited into the bedroom.

"Please sit here on the bed so we can have a conversation," Steve said.

I sat as close to the edge as possible, pulling at my robe to stay covered. I was completely naked underneath. I don't want to be here.

What am I doing? How can I get out of this gracefully? I feel uncomfortable. Who do I think I am? And then a deeper part of me knew it was where I needed to be at that moment in my life. You have something to learn here. You are safe. Trust the process. Trust.

Vera, Steve's wife, joined us on the bed. I relaxed more with her sweet energy.

"What would you like to accomplish today, Wendy?" Steve asked.

I was confused by Steve's question. I was thinking it was pretty obvious why I was there. Why is he asking me this? He's the expert.

"I don't know exactly how to answer that question," I said. "Because I don't know what to expect or even what's possible for me today. Isn't it obvious why I am here? Doesn't everyone else schedule a session with you for the same reason?"

Steve explained that some people just want to talk and get information.

"Oh. Well I'm here for a sensual session at the recommendation of my friend Sheila. This is a gift to myself."

I really didn't want to waste time talking. I wanted to get right down to business.

"So are you ready to get started then?" Steve asked.

With a big breath I said, "Yes", even though I was also feeling a bit uneasy. I thought to myself, "*Am I really doing this?*"

Vera said, "Wendy, would you like me to go first and give you a demonstration, so you can watch closely and get an idea of what is possible for you? You will also see what your experience will be like."

"Yes," I quickly responded. Hell yeah, I was thinking.

Steve leaned his back against the pillows along the headboard and sat in an upright position. He placed another pillow by his right leg and a towel next to it.

I watched Vera lean on the pillow and place her buttocks on the towel. Then she gracefully moved her long blouse up her body, exposing her pussy.

Steve put on gloves and dipped his right index finger into lubricant. Then he placed his left hand under her butt as an anchor.

Vera opened her legs.

Steve gently moved the lips of Vera's labia to the side. Her body immediately began to move in a rhythmic wave. Wow. I could sense energy flowing through her.

Vera moaned.

This was a woman in her pleasure. No doubt about that, I thought.

Steve said "Look closely. Can you see how Vera's pussy is engorged?"

"Yes, I see that."

The lips of her labia were glistening. Lit up. I saw sparkly purple and red hues. They were thicker … like lips that have been injected with collagen, only this was nature's collagen. Steve then touched Vera's clit and gently rubbed it. Vera's mouth parted into a smile, and her face was glowing. She suddenly looked younger. It was like the full-bodied orgasm was aging her backwards.

As Steve stroked Vera's clit, I was even feeling turned on in my body. I was wet. I wanted my turn.

"Wow. I'm mesmerized," I said. I observed her body fully receive her orgasm for several minutes.

"OK, Wendy, have you seen enough of what is possible, and are you ready?"

"Yes, I'm ready. That's why I'm here!" I said.

Steve placed the palm of his right hand on Vera's pubic bone to bring her down from her orgasm. Vera took a deep breath and smiled as she repositioned her blouse and moved to the side so that I could have my experience.

Steve took off his gloves and put on a new pair. He then placed a new towel onto the bed and told me to place my butt on the towel and then lie down. I did as I was told, still wondering if I was brave enough to go through with it.

"Can you open your robe?" Steve asked. This is not a time to be shy, I was thinking. "Now relax and open your legs."

I opened my legs.

"Please relax," he said again.

I was finding it difficult to allow my body to soften.

"You're doing well, Wendy. Are you comfortable?"

"Yes," I said.

"We are going to communicate openly so I can get feedback on what you are experiencing and so that you can get practice telling me what feels good. OK?"

"Yes." I said again.

"I'm applying lubricant to my finger now."

"OK." I said.

"I am going to touch you now. Are you ready?"

"Yes."

I felt the lubricant on my clit, and then he began stroking. Light, slow strokes. Just on my clit. Immediately I began to feel a sweet energy in my genitals. I was experiencing my orgasm, but still feeling a tiny bit shy to speak up. He really does know what he is doing, I thought.

None of it felt sexual. Instead, it felt sensual. I kept my focus on the waves of pleasure coming from my pussy as I reminded myself I was safe. Suddenly, the sensations stopped. I thought my orgasm was over.

"Stop resisting," Steve said.

"I'm not resisting," I said.

"Yes you are."

"No I'm not!"

"Yes you are. Vera can you observe more closely?"

Vera moved her eyes close to my pussy and watched very intently.

I realized I was arguing with experts. Maybe I needed to trust them.

As Steve stroked my clit. I noticed my resistance. I started to feel frustrated.

"What do you think, Vera? Is Wendy resisting?"

"Do that again, Steve," Vera said instructing him to continue a stroke. She was researching my orgasm.

Steve stroked my clit again. My body resisted again. I was protecting myself.

Steve and Vera discussed my orgasm as he stroked and she observed. There was something very serious about their conversation, yet I could find the humor in it, too, as I lay between them, legs splayed open in my too-small silk robe.

The Bodanskys both agreed. I was resisting going into a deeper and longer orgasm.

My orgasm was stopping short of something spectacular like I'd witnessed with Vera. For decades I'd thought that my short, quick orgasms were normal. Now I knew I was resisting feeling more. I wondered, what else in my life could I have been resisting all these years? I took a breath into my core as Steve's finger met my clit again with another long, slow stroke. Relaxing into the touch this time, I felt more pulsing throughout my genitals. It was a glimpse of what I could experience on the other side of my resistance. Just the awareness of my resistance had shifted my orgasm ever so slightly.

The time passed so quickly. It was time to end my session. Steve let me know he was going to bring me down from my orgasm; he then placed his hand on my pubic bone for several minutes. I could feel the pulsation in my pussy slow down. It took several minutes. I pulled the robe around me, and Steve helped me to a sitting position.

I took a deep breath and looked at Vera who was next to me on the bed.

"How do you feel, Wendy?" she asked.

"I feel good… a little disappointed, but that's ok," I said.

With her kind eyes, Vera smiled at me very lovingly and said, "Now you have information." I nodded my head and agreed. I felt grateful for the session with Vera and Steve and the new knowledge I had about myself, my body and my orgasm, and what was possible.

There was a bit of a letdown after I left. So that's it, I thought. My orgasm is a sneeze. All these years, I'd thought that was my orgasm. Well it is my orgasm, only I thought that was all there was to an orgasm. And now I learn there is more. What will experiencing a full body orgasm be like for me? Is it possible for me? What has to happen inside of me? What type of transformation must take place in order for me to experience an extended massive orgasm like Vera's, instead of the sneeze? I kept remembering what Vera said as she looked at me with her eyes full of love, "Now you have information."

I wondered what I was going to do with this new information.

When I returned to Houston, I made an appointment with Jim, the therapist who had helped me to heal from sexual abuse. I wanted to share my experience, especially since he tried many times over the years to help me connect to what he called my "sexual body". It was his way of helping me to connect to my sensual bliss. I never quite got what he meant until I took the session with the Bodanskys. Now I asked Jim for guidance on transforming my resistance to feeling more of my orgasm. Jim suggested we go into the room where he does his energy healing work. He asked me to relax on the massage table. As he started to guide me through a meditation, I felt peace in my body. He moved his hand to just above my genitals and kept it there for several minutes. He finally spoke.

"I feel stagnant energy here, like water in a pond that is not moving. How about you start imagining the water flowing here?" I did my best but didn't feel any different.

After the session ended, I continued with his idea over the next twenty-four hours. I found I was having fun playing the visualizations without any expectation of an outcome.

Instead of imagining water flowing, I imagined waterfalls flowing. I imagined several waterfalls flowing. I began visualizing the waterfalls of Maui flowing in my pussy.

The next day I relaxed on my bed and began reading one of my erotica books. I had only read a few pages when I felt my body start moving, like the waves of the ocean. I was moving in a rhythmic motion of hip thrusts as if I was having sex, but I had not touched my body at all.

I felt the pleasurable pulsing of the muscles inside my pussy just as if my heart was beating right there. It was in flow with my hips. Rapture.

I was wet. I was turned on. I felt freedom and joy. *Wow! What is happening?* I was in a blissful state of shock and surprise.

I allowed myself to experience my orgasm for hours. I realized that my body was experiencing a full body orgasm just like the one I observed Vera demonstrating in my sensual session. I was mesmerized with my own body and its ability to experience this deep level of ecstasy. And then I remembered.

My orgasm is me, and that part of me was too scared to express itself. My orgasm had been locked away for nearly fifty years, too afraid to come out. I was programmed to feel shame about my God-given gift that all women have. At a young age I equated feeling my orgasm with death. But in truth, not feeling my orgasm fully was a slow death. I had no chance to live into this part of my femininity until I unleashed my orgasm.

I didn't need a man to be turned on. I didn't need a man to experience a full body orgasm.

I reclaimed my power. I liberated my orgasm. I am free.

About the Author
Wendy G. Young

www.wendygyoung.com

What did you want to be when you were eight years old?

I wanted to be an artist. After starting my healing journey 20 years later I began painting. I discovered that my depth of inner healing is directly related to the level of creativity and art I produce. This motivates me to help others heal and reconnect to their creativity.

If you could give one piece of advice to your younger self about your orgasm, what would it be?

Love and cherish your orgasm no matter what anyone may say to you about it. There might be a time in your life when you do not feel safe to fully feel your orgasm. Remember that your orgasm is there for you when you are ready to really know her. She is yours and nobody can ever take her from you. Stay in communication with your orgasm even when you do not feel her. There will be a time when you will fully explore her magnificence. Show love to your orgasm by speaking to her kindly, touching her softly and laughing with her while living your life full out. Your orgasm is your divine source of all good and will respond to your love by bringing you health and happiness in all areas of your life. Always believe in her miracle.

If your orgasm had a voice, what would your orgasm say to you about the piece you wrote for this book?

You are brilliant and courageous in your storytelling. I feel liberated in your words and feelings, and I am celebrating you for openly sharing the journey you traveled to get to know me. Thank you for bringing in your playful child who knew who she was as a divine being and that she needed to protect herself by forgetting about me until she felt safe. I was waiting to feel loved and cherished, and I do. I know that others will feel safe to know and explore their orgasm because of your willingness to do the inner healing work and follow your intuition to write about me. I am deeply grateful to you for your gift, and I am sending you many blessings.

Author's Note: In the writing of my story I use the word "pussy" to honor my sensual journey and the teachings of Regena Thomashauer at Mama Gena's School of Womanly Arts. Pussy invokes the reawakening and connection to our divine feminine essence.

THIRTEEN

*"Remembering that you are going to die is the best way
I know to avoid the trap of thinking you have
something to lose. You are already naked.*

There is no reason not to follow your heart."

—Steve Jobs

CLAIMING MY ORGASM
by Charmaine Mitchell

It was summer in Toronto and we were out for a girls' night when Sonya asked me, "So, do you think you will have sex with only your husband for the rest of your life?"

Before I knew it, the words "Hell no!" flew powerfully past my lips. The words surprised my head, but not my body. My body was speaking.

With an amused smirk on her gorgeous full lips, Sonya continued her witchy stirring of the cauldron: "So who from your past would you have sex with if you could?"

"JAMES!" I blurted out.

What?! Where did that come from? My head struggled to understand. How is it that this woman whom I'd met only two weeks earlier can pull this information out of me that I had never spoken out loud?

James...

We met when I was twenty years old in Vancouver, BC. It was 1991, and James was my manager at a place called the Cactus Club where I was a server. I was also a flirt. He responded to my flirtation with a note written on a cocktail napkin. He passed it to another server to hand to me as I was cleaning up. It said that he had been imagining the things that he would like to do to me. My body responded: *Hmmmmm, this is intriguing, let's check this out.* I looked back across the restaurant at him, and smiled.

We didn't date or have a relationship of any kind. Both of us were afraid of relationships and getting hurt. There wasn't a lot of communication between us. We had sex. Twice.

I remember there was something about his touch that felt familiar, knowing and electric. It didn't make sense in my head, but my body responded to him. I wanted more, but when he called me "forward" because I enjoyed flirting with guys, I could feel a pang in my stomach, like a punch. I felt I was being judged, that my "being forward" was unacceptable. My behavior at work changed after that comment, especially around him. I shut down. When James started dating another girl a month later and she became pregnant, I knew it was really over.

This was not the first time I had been judged "wrong" for my flirtatious behavior. I learned to alter my behavior around certain people and to wear a different mask instead of being myself. It was a pattern that I continued into my marriage. Fast forward nearly twenty years later, and my body was remembering his touch. What was going on? I had to find out.

About a week after Sonya sparked my desire, I searched and found James on Facebook. I told him I wanted him again. He said two words: "When?" and "Where?"

We wrote back and forth, making plans to see each other. Through his words, I could feel his passion, and I knew he could feel mine. We explored ourselves deeply and exposed ourselves to one another. And then something unexpected happened – we fell in love, and I knew then that he had always loved me. My heart skipped a beat when he wrote, "I remember you all those years ago in a sundress, laughing, and your beauty took my breath away."

New York City, January...

I was so excited. James was on his way from the airport. We had agreed to meet on the streets of New York City. I was standing outside Barnes & Noble at 66th and Broadway in a fur coat with only lingerie underneath when it began to snow. I looked up to enjoy the magic of snowflakes falling on my face and missed his cab pulling up. He came up from behind me, turned me around, grabbed the back of my head and planted a kiss on my mouth. "Holy shit!" I yelled out. This was really happening. My whole body was clear and grounded, knowing that this felt so RIGHT.

We walked to the apartment in a state of nervous, excited energy, catching stolen glimpses of each other as we chatted. When we walked into the apartment, he smiled at the music I already had playing. It was songs that we had been sharing back and forth for the past several months. He stood looking into my eyes, and then slowly we undressed each other and began touching, like nervous teenagers. I kissed his back, gently brushing my lips across his skin, inhaling his scent. I could sense our nervousness – I wanted to push quickly through this moment, so that we could relax into the weekend, but I also wanted to savor each touch, each kiss as all the built-up anticipation and passion between us was set free.

The next morning, when James held up my coat for me to put on, I started to cry. He asked why, and I told him my husband hadn't held my coat out for me during our entire marriage. As we walked the streets of New York City together that day, James took my hand, something else my husband never wanted to do. He remembered my favorite food and my favorite drinks, and he reminded of me of things that I had forgotten. It began to dawn on me that when I had finally decided to treasure myself, I called in a man who wanted to treasure me, too.

On our final morning together, after we finished making love, he listened to me as I chatted about life. I felt so loved, so seen and so heard by this man. He was so present with me. As I continued talking, he slowly caressed my skin. I loved the sensation of his fingers gliding across my body. I mentioned that it was a new experience for me. He didn't say anything. He just looked at me with his sparkly green eyes and started to make his way back down between my legs. I couldn't believe he was going down there. He had already spent more hours licking my pussy then I had ever experienced in my life. It seemed like the hundredth time in two days. I took a deep breath and surrendered, again.

This time I felt new sensations in my body. There was a tingling in my arms and legs that was shooting from the heat in my pussy. It felt electrical. Then all of a sudden, a sound that I had never heard myself make escaped from a primitive place inside me. It was a guttural sound – loud and long. Involuntary spasms took over my arms and legs. It's as though I was out of my body, and yet I couldn't have been more in my body.

I jumped off the bed. "What did you just do to me?" I kept asking it over and over.

He responded, "I just loved you."

I stood in front of him, naked and crying.

He asked, "Was that your first orgasm?"

I didn't know, of course, because I had never experienced one. But yes, it was my first clitoral orgasm. I had followed my body's wisdom, and it led me to my awakening. I was thirty-nine years old.

For the longest time, I really thought it was the guy. I was in love with James for loving me the way he did. Yes, of course it was beautiful – it felt amazing to receive love like that. Yet, as the years passed, patterns similar to those in my marriage showed up in the relationship with James. He wasn't as present with me, he was distracted, his attention waned. This was surprising and shocking. I felt disillusioned. How could this be happening? In my marriage, my husband loved me by providing financially, but he couldn't show up for me in other ways, like being present. I resented him for not being able to show up, and I found him lacking. I thought that my happiness was his responsibility and was what marriage was all about. I looked long and hard inside myself. I realized that I had made my happiness James' responsibility by connecting my orgasm to him. I also came to the conclusion that until I dealt with this co-dependent behavior, it would keep showing up in every relationship.

Both men loved me and showed up for me the best they could. As soon as I decided that I'd had enough of my needs going unmet in my marriage, I called in a man to show up for me in the ways I desired. James took the time to see me. What I said mattered to him, and it mattered to me that he listened. It cracked my heart wide open and led to my orgasm. But I found myself relying on his attention as validation of my worthiness to be loved. When James' attention waned, I called on myself to show up for me.

I have come to see that when I saw myself, listened to myself and honored what my voice had to say, I cracked my own heart open. My orgasm belongs to me. And I am still in love. This time it is with myself.

About the Author
Charmaine Mitchell

www.charmainemitchell.com

What did you want to be when you were eight years old?

I wanted to be a famous actress when I was eight years old.

If you could give one piece of advice to your younger self about your orgasm, what would it be?

Love yourself and treat your body as the temple that it is. Treasure yourself and others will treasure you. Never settle for less. Your orgasm is your responsibility, not a man's. The journey to your orgasm is love, self-love.

If your orgasm had a voice, what would your orgasm say to you about the piece you wrote for this book?

My orgasm would say thank you.

FOURTEEN

"Surrender to your Divine blueprint."

—Marilene Isaacs

Jamie —

Thank you for helping me birth this story and for being a witness to so many things that most people never believe. You are so amazing. Being of light and such a wonderful friend —

love
Darlene

I WAS BORN ORGASMIC
by Marilene Isaacs Kauffman

I remember my birth, but I also remember where I was before birth.
Before I emerged from my mother's womb, I remember there was light,
there was joy, there was oneness. There was no separation, only the
rhythmic movement of life. I remember feeling safe. And then I emerged
from the oneness, and I felted tricked, sad and alone. It was 4.42am on
November 5th, 1948.

During that time, it was a popular practice to give the mother ether
to knock her out during the birthing process. After I emerged, there were
huge, bright lights and people in masks and gowns. And then I saw her –
the vessel that I had been one with and felt safe in. She was lying there –
no movement, no co-creating with these alien, faceless, masked strangers.
I thought she was dead.

My father said he knew I was going to be a girl, and my name was to
be Marilene. Joy, my middle name, was chosen to honor my mother,
whose name was Joyce.

I was born into the legacy of a mystical family. My paternal great
grandmother, Serilda Emilene Shook Moore, was of the Creek Nation,
one of the five civilized tribes in America. She and my grandmother were
very spiritual, intuitive and had healing abilities. From a young age, I was
already showing mine.

As a young child, I always felt like a huge person – like I was in
many places at one time. For me there was no separation in time or space.
That's why I was at first confused when I was born. I felt a separation
from the oneness I remembered before my birth.

My mother was very spiritual, which was different from being
religious. She had graduated from Central College, a very small Dutch

Reformed College in Pella, Iowa, in 1943. When she graduated, my mother wanted to be a missionary for the Dutch Reformed Church in China. World War II was going on, so instead they sent her to Jackson County, Kentucky, to teach at a boarding school that the church had started for the poor kids. Mother also worked for the Red Cross, and that is where she met my wild and handsome father. James Boyd Isaacs was seven years older than my mother, had a third-grade education and for a while had been a moonshine runner. My mother fell in love with him. After they married, they moved to Indiana where I was born a few years later, in a small town with only 15,000 residents.

My father was a beekeeper. His first swarm of bees came to him when he was five years old, which was a strong indication of the magnetic energy that ran in our family. I remember being in the garden with my mother one day as she looked up at a bee on a flower. She said that the bees and the flowers loved each other and worked together to create life. As she spoke, I felt the electrical and magnetic energy of the universe in orgasmic union. I always felt the union from the God within , and God felt to me like what I now understand through Buddhist teachings to be Yab Yum, the father and the mother in union, creating life. It reminded me I was of heaven and earth. Even after birth, I remembered I was never separated from the unconditional love of the holy spirit.

As a child, I could remember the past and see the future. We went to church three times a week. Once, my Sunday school teacher was talking about Jesus, whom I remembered as Yeshua, and Mary and Mary Magdalene. I had vivid recall of them and of the times the teacher was speaking of, but the story she was telling was wrong. I got very upset with her when she said Mary Magdalene was a prostitute. I remember Mary Magdalene. She was a disciple and the wife of Yeshua. They worked together to teach and to heal. When I protested to the teacher that Mary Magdalene was not a prostitute, the Sunday school teacher promptly grabbed me and spanked. I was four.

I started my period when I was ten, a much younger age than for most girls. I was so excited because my body felt electrified and blissful. Looking back, I would say I was orgasmic. I was so happy, I told my mother to tell my father. I went to school and told my friends. I wanted everyone to know! I announced my news to a friend at school, and she said, "You are a woman now."

Growing up, I was in a constant state of ecstasy. Any slight movement while in class would bring on amazing, full body rushes that I now know to be orgasm, but at the time, I didn't know anything about sex. I thought it was normal for my body to feel blissful all the time!

When I was in the seventh grade, I was leaning against the wall at the end of the hall, outside of a classroom. A boy came along and pulled my legs out from under me; I landed on the concrete floor with a direct hit on my tail bone. I saw stars, and I felt myself leave my body as it filled with light. When I dropped back into my body, I felt the extreme sensation at my tailbone of an awakening and of a closing down. In an instant I went from ecstasy into agony. I went from feeling happy and outspoken to being silenced. In that moment, my life changed. I literally fell out of the union from within, into the illusion of separation. I was flooded with fear, shame and embarrassment.

For the next couple of years, I could hardly get into and out of chairs, but I kept the pain to myself. I was trapped in my body with it. I found out years later, after having extensive cranial-sacral work, that I have one of the strangest and most broken tail bones the doctor had ever seen. It sticks out, like a tail.

I wasn't really allowed to date in high school. Sometimes I went out with guys, but mostly I thought men didn't find me attractive. I went off to college in Iowa, to the same school that my mother attended, even though my body was telling me to move to New York City. In college, my first real physical intimacy with a boyfriend was very strange and uneventful. I had remembered before birth the feeling of cosmic orgasm, so I soon realized that I was destined to be on a different journey than others in regard to relationships and dating. The healing of my body continued as I met and married the man who would father my son and as I launched myself as a psychic and healer working with people all over the US. Unlike my own birth, when I thought my mother was dead, when I gave birth to my son, Merlin, I chose to be present, awake, alive and an orgasmic participant.

After my son was born, I started to fully drop into my body again and to feel safe. One day when Merlin was about eighteen months old, I was in a grocery store with my husband and him. I suddenly came to an abrupt stop and leaned on the grocery cart as a full body kundalini experience manifested. The switch had been turned back on. I had awakened to the memory of the divine alchemical marriage with the inner beloved, where we live in a constant state of union and orgasm. The cosmos' kundalini energy was back.

A few years after my kundalini awakening, I took a trip with Merlin and his dad to Hueston Woods near Oxford, Ohio. It was winter, and we had lots of snow, so we went there to get away because they had an indoor pool. I was going through another level of healing and awakening at that time, as well. I had been very activated about my childhood and the broken tail bone, so I was doing inner work on forgiving and understanding it all. I had dreams that night, and when it came time to drive back to Indianapolis the next day, instead of going on the main roads, I said we needed to drive the back roads and go through Connersville, my home town. By the time we got there, no one was on the streets because of the blizzard. When we stopped to get gas, another car pulled up to get gas, as well. I looked up to see a man getting out of his car, wearing a high school letter jacket from my high school. To my amazement, it was the boy, now the man, who had pulled my legs out from under me all those years ago. In that present moment, the pain, shame, anger and depression disappeared, and my heart and body filled with the healing power of unconditional love. I had awakened again to the oneness within myself.

About the Author
Marilene Isaacs Kauffman

www.centerofpeace.com

What did you want to be when you were eight years old?

When I was eight years old, I would have been in the third grade going into the fourth grade, and I just wanted to be whatever I wanted to be in that moment. Sometimes I wanted to be an actress, but I didn't have to act. It was just my way of being my true, authentic self. I remember wanting to be glamorous – I was always putting on make-up and wearing my mother's high heels. She was a great seamstress and would make very special outfits for me for every holiday.

I had special powers and knowledge beyond what most eight year olds had. I created altars and put things on them. Sometimes I felt very sad, and my mother asked me why I was crying. I would say, "Because my Soul Mate isn't on this Earth."

About that same time, I became very aware of wanting male company and attention, in a bonding way, because the girls were very mean and jealous of me. I continued to be glamorous, but I was also a tomboy. I was not afraid of climbing trees, and I learned to play softball to connect with male energy. Even back then, I wanted to be what I was and always have been, a very balanced male/female. I wanted to be a person, and I had an overwhelming desire to be me.

What would you say to your younger self about orgasm?

My younger self was experiencing kundalini all the time, so the piece of advice that I would give would be this: You are already complete, from within. You can have a cosmic orgasm constantly, so pay attention to who and what you are attracting to yourself to join with in the physical level of sexual connection.

When you have sex with someone, they become you, you become them. You take on their karma, and they take on yours. Choose wisely and organically who to connect with for orgasm. And remember that some of the most powerful orgasms ever may be thinking about or connecting with another, not physically but energetically.

In every moment, you are the spark of life that is the eternal flame of transmutation, the perpetual energy that creates and destroys. You are constantly creating new worlds and new stars.

Anything else?

Even at the age of 4, when I shouted out in protest to the Sunday School teacher saying Mary Magdalene was a prostitute, what I really said was "No, I wasn't." I didn't say it that way because I didn't want to sound egotistical so I said, "No she wasn't", but the truth is the energy of judgement and harshness against the divine feminine was so harsh in the fundamentalist Baptist Church that even at that young age it went to the heart of me and awakened me out of the illusion of separation, and into the remembrance of the union with the Beloved. It also brought a profound sadness that I carried for a long time.

As a young woman, I would tell my mother that my Soul Mate was not on Earth. I would build altars outside and put flowers and pray for the return of my Soul Mate, always feeling him inside yet longing for his physical presence. I know now that I was reliving, and remembering what I experienced in the incarnation of Mary Magdalene. I am a firm believer that famous people in history are made up of a group Soul and that I was one of many who chose to join to manifest the archetype of Mary Magdalene. My Father knew I was going to be a girl, and made my name up—Marilene—another clue to my lineage.

I remember how powerful it was to know and experience the redemption of Sophia and how Jesus, Christos The Light freed the captured and defiled divine feminine restoring her, to her rightful place. Think about the last 2,000 years of Christianity, if it had been based on a married couple, who had children, who were equals and who knew the mysteries and explained them. They healed, taught and actualized the unconditional love that joined two bloodlines to bring restoration and redemption to all. Instead, this was hidden, and the dark energy created the age old myth of the dying, sacrificed god, born of a virgin and sexless.

Jesus came to bring a state of grace, not to continue the need for death and blood sacrifice.

So I now understand and have always known, remembered and as a spiritual teacher taught from memory the divine blueprint, rather than the lie. The awakening that is happening now to the masses is amazing. We are remembering who we really are and healing the illusion of separation that occurred when we fell through fear into guilt and shame. We are realigning with the true frequency of unconditional love. When you choose to go deep into the truth and feeling the union with the Beloved, you will vibrate and feel the continual orgasmic, true OM of the Universe in every cell of your Being.

FIFTEEN

"Sexuality is one of the ways that we become enlightened actually, because it leads us to self-knowledge."

—Alice Walker

FINDING AMRITA
by Jennifer Lakshmi Dove-Robinson

I can see him now with his red beard and curly hair, tall and thin.
He wore his hair kind of long, like an '80s rocker. He always wore khaki
pants and button-down shirts. His locker was near mine, up on the top
floor near the psychology classrooms. He was only 17 when we met. He
seemed older than the other boys. I was starting 10th grade. Jeffrey was in
12th. There was something about the way he looked at me that made me
wonder, who is this guy?

My family had recently moved to the area. At my previous school, in
an affluent county in Pennsylvania, the Sebago Docksiders shoes and
brightly-colored polo shirts that the kids wore bewildered me. I didn't
own Jordache jeans or Calvin Klein blazers. Consequently, I was shuffled
in with the other new kids who didn't play lacrosse or field hockey, kids
who felt as lost there as I did. So I when came to this new school in the
middle of a rural area full of working farms, I was relieved. I was
convinced that it would take less effort to find a friend.

Jeffrey kept coming around my locker. I wondered if he had learned
my schedule, as he seemed to show up at the same time I did every day.
And, finally, one afternoon after school, he walked over to my locker,
where I was grabbing books for my homework. He pushed his hair back
behind his right ear, looked down at his Converse All Star shoes and said,
"Hi, I'm Jeffrey. Um, do you want to go out?"

My answer was, "Out where?" as I didn't understand at first that he
was interested in a date.

"Out out," he said. "You know, out to a movie or something."

"Oh!" I said, "Yes, but I have to ask my Dad." My first date. Dad
had always said that my sister and I couldn't start dating until we were at

least 16. I was only 15. It took some doing, but I managed to convince him that going to dinner and a movie with a new friend was not a date.

We didn't have a whole lot in common, but there was electricity between us, and we were both interested in finding out about the other. I could feel his pulse as I held his strong hand. While looking into a mirrored wall at the movie theater, we discovered that our eyes were nearly the same color. We spent hours talking on the phone at night after school even though we had seen each other many times during the day. He gave me a copy of Viktor Frankl's book, *Man's Search for Meaning*, which was like food to me. A godsend, for sure. I had shared with Jeffrey that my mother was alcoholic and that my family life was extremely chaotic. That book sent me on my quest toward hopeful self-discovery. I have Jeffrey to thank for that. And so, we went on our not-a-date, and I tried Chinese food for the first time in my life with him.

Within a couple of weeks after our first date, the subject of sex came up.

"Do you want to… um…?"

"All the way? Yes, do you?"

"Do you think we're ready?"

"Almost."

His mother worked. Instead of taking my bus home, Jeffrey picked me up near the back entrance of the school in his green Toyota Supra. Somehow I had convinced my mom that his mother would be home when Jeffrey took me over to hang out at his house. I also convinced her that we were just watching television and doing homework. Instead, we were making out like fiends. I loved his thin body. And, I think, he loved mine. When he mentioned that his older brother thought I still had my baby fat, though, I immediately began to diet my way down to 110 pounds. Still, I loved being so close to someone whose body was so foreign to me. I loved rolling around on the couch with him and kissing for hours and hours.

Then came the day that we decided to go all the way. He was a nervous wreck. I, on the other hand, was calm as a lake. I was so excited and wanted it and him so badly. We first tried condoms. Who knew it would take a few frustrated tries over a few frustrating afternoons for him to enter me? It was over quickly, and he cried because he thought he was hurting me. He was, but only for a minute, and then the door opened into bliss. It felt strange having something inside my body that had nothing to do with me, yet I wanted him there so much.

And so we practiced. A lot.

In the hours before my midnight curfew, we used to go out parking in this abandoned cornfield after dark, bright stars in the sky. We'd roll the windows down and listen to make sure no one was nearby. Fresh air filled the car. We'd kiss and kiss as if the night was endless. Then I'd roll toward him and, leaving my clothes behind, climb on top of him, adjusting my legs to skirt the gear shift. I'd ride him to within an inch of his life, as if he was there, passive in the driver's seat, purely for my own pleasure. He didn't seem to mind in the least. I think he was initially surprised that I was such an active participant. I loved every minute of it. I allowed myself to open to the experience. It was the most freedom I'd ever felt in my body and the closest to God I'd felt up until that point in my life.

We never did much beyond me on top of him or him on top of me, except for oral sex, which was just for him. The topic of oral sex for me never emerged as an option.

Sex was blissful, but the anxiety around unprotected sex was dreadful. We were using condoms, but now Jeffrey was pushing me to go on the pill. But how? Neither of us had any information, nor did we know where to go to get information. I found out that Jeffrey was asking his boss a lot of questions about what kind of birth control I should be on. That was an uncomfortable discovery. In the end, I went along with the idea of going on birth control pills. I wasn't clear that this was what I wanted, but I was also nervous as a cat, raised to please people, and curious for more experience with sex. I knew I didn't want to get pregnant, but it was really the furthest thing from my mind. There was no Planned Parenthood in my town. Where could I go?

My first step was to make an appointment with my pediatrician. Jeffrey dropped me off at the door of the office. My pediatrician said that if I really wanted to go on birth control pills I'd have to have a vaginal exam. He said he didn't do many of those as a pediatrician. "I appreciate that you and your boyfriend want to be safe," he said, "but Jenny, you're way too young, and I don't feel right not telling your parents as you're under age." But in the end, he agreed. I underwent my first vaginal exam with a male doctor, my pediatrician, whom I had only seen for two other appointments. It was the first time I'd ever been to a doctor without my mother. I'm sure I left my body during that exam. I can remember the doctor trying repeatedly to talk me out of taking the pills, out of having sex. I was 15. I didn't even drive yet.

I went on the pill. I filled the prescriptions myself. I hid the pills in a hatbox in my closet and took them every morning like a good girl.

Sex was a kind of refuge. It was a place where I could be myself and explore myself. It was a place where I could learn what another person thought, felt, and dreamt. Jeffrey also introduced me to marijuana and hash, which I loved almost as much as I loved sex. We lay around smoking pot after making love, talking, and making food together before he drove me home. I'd never been intimate in any deep way with anyone until Jeffrey. It was also a way to escape the craziness and unpredictability of my home life. Being with someone who professed to love me, who was gentle with me, helped me to understand that I could hope for more in my life than waiting around for my mom to stop drinking or hoping that the near-daily dramas at home would stop happening.

It turns out that Jeffrey was not only my first lover, he was also my most conservative lover, perhaps because of the pressure he put on himself to get it right. One afternoon while having sex, I, who had always been easily orgasmic with my clothes on, rolling around on the couch with Jeffrey while we kissed, was now able to reach orgasm with him inside me. O, holy wonderful. But later that week, everything changed.

"You peed in my bed!" he yelled, mad as hell, pulling out of me as he jumped up from his bed. "You've peed all over my bed! Get the hell up and get out of here so I can clean this up."

"I did not!" I said, but I wasn't sure. What had just come out of me? I was still new at this sex business, and so was he. We'd had sex together only about ten times by then. There was no ammonia smell, no telltale yellow stain. The liquid was clear, like water, and it didn't smell much at all, but I felt shame down to my core. It enveloped me; my skin became hot, my face red. I gathered my clothes and went into the bathroom. Splashing water on my face, I looked at myself in the mirror. Did I just pee during sex? Was that even possible?

When I came out of the bathroom fully clothed, Jeffrey was stripping the sheets off his bed. "I can't even believe that you did that!" he yelled "I've got to get this cleaned up before my mom gets home."

"I'm sorry," I said. It was all I could think to say.

Together, we put his sheets in the washer. He had stopped speaking to me by then. Silent treatments are the worst kind of punishment, and I didn't even know exactly what had happened. We both assumed it was my fault. He drove me home in complete silence. I didn't receive a phone call from him that night.

A few weeks later, I developed a urinary tract infection. It was relentless and constant. The pain was agonizing. I ended up seeing a urologist who did a lot of tests. He started me on antibiotics. When those didn't seem to make a difference, he met with me one afternoon after school and patiently suggested I opt for an outpatient procedure called urethral stricture to try and stretch my urethra. I agreed, along with my mom's support, to try this surgery. At the hospital, early in the morning before the procedure, the urologist and his staff performed a uroflowmetry test. They filled my system with intravenous saline, and I had to drink copious amounts of water that tasted like metallic pipes. It took me forever to pee all that liquid out. During the uroflowmetry test, the urologist was on the other side of the room behind a curtain, monitoring my output on a computer. He said, "Jenny, you pee like an old woman."

"I'm trying," I said.

"You have to let it go," he said. "You have to trust that it's supposed to come out. Trust me."

But I didn't trust him. I was 16 by this time. When I went to see him for my next appointment, he was more than a little inappropriate with me. There was always a nurse present in the room during my examinations, but still, one day, as he poked around with his head under the paper sheet that covered my body, he asked, "Are you a virgin?" I looked at the female nurse who was holding my hand. I was a good girl. I was raised to be nice, to be sweetness incarnate. No matter how I felt, I was not to make a scene, not to get angry. In my family, only my mother was allowed to get angry.

The nurse said to me, "It's okay, you can answer."

In my mind, I'm thinking, Really? Is this pertinent to my problem? But I heard myself say "Yes", which wasn't true and hadn't been true for a while.

His next words from under the sheet were, "Well, honey, your husband is going to be in for such a treat. He'll never leave you. You have the tightest little vagina I've ever examined."

I thought I was going to die. I looked at the nurse, who rolled her eyes and squeezed my hand. When he came out from under the sheet, the doctor said, "Learn how to relax and let yourself feel, let yourself urinate when you need to. Don't hold it; don't try to keep it in longer than you have to. That's my advice. I don't think there's anything else I can do for you, Miss Dove."

I was shaking with anger, feeling strangely violated, lightheaded, and nauseated. I was confused, because was that supposed to be a compliment? Wasn't it exactly none of his fucking business?

I never went back. And I never told anyone.

However, I was furious. I was angry with my boyfriend for shaming me and angry with my body for peeing during sex. Looking back, of course I developed those chronic urinary tract infections because someone I loved told me there was something wrong with the way my body expressed itself sexually. What I began to realize, at the core of my being, is that there was nothing wrong with me.

I was surrounded by a pack of men who were all weighing in on what was right and best for me. Even Jeffrey had talked to his boss about birth control instead of talking to me first. The boss had opinions, Jeffrey's brother had opinions, my pediatrician had opinions, and now this creepy urologist had opinions. Everybody had opinions. And, all the while, my opinion was the only one that mattered.

I never had that experience with Jeffrey again. Although sex with him was still great, that part of my body had closed up shop for a while.

Jeffrey asked me to marry him during the summer after he graduated from high school. I was 16 years old and getting ready to enter the 11th grade. He wanted to know if I would say yes and then wait the two years until I graduated from high school and then wait again until he had his Associates degree from the community college.

What? Married? How could I know if I wanted to marry anyone? I didn't want to marry anyone. Yet, here was this great guy trying to get me pinned into place in order to make his life complete. It felt like the same story all over again. A man's opinion about what was best for me seemed to be taking up all the airspace in my life.

I knew that college was ahead of me, because it seemed like the right idea. I was 16, hardly worldly, very shy, and quiet. Even at 16, though, I knew for a fact that marriage was not what I wanted. Marriage was the projected path my parents had envisioned for me. To marry a high school sweetheart, just as they had done, was the extent of what they'd imagined I'd want for my life. To be honest, the pressure of Jeffrey's question was overwhelming. I probably didn't handle it with grace. I broke up with him. In the end, it was really just about nine months that we were together.

It wasn't until many years later, after many lovers and during my marriage, that I began to read about Tantra while studying to be a yoga teacher. This was when I first learned about the phenomenon known by the Sanskrit word, Amrita. I learned that women can and do ejaculate during orgasm. Once in a while, I would feel that sensation of extra fluid during orgasm, but I tried not to make a big deal about it. It was still a bit embarrassing. Luckily, none of my other lovers ever said a word about it. It was good to finally learn definitively that I was not weird. Thank god! According to Carolyn Muir and other teachers of Tantra, Amrita is considered the sacred fluid of the Feminine Divine that, yes, does seep, or pour, through the urethra during a peak sexual experience. It doesn't happen for every woman, and it doesn't happen every time for the women who experience it.

In the winter of 1994, I went to the Kripalu Center for Yoga and Health to pursue certification as a yoga instructor. This is where I heard the phrase "female ejaculation" for the first time. I dropped to my knees to give thanks to my body and to try and forgive my uneducated younger self and my equally uneducated first lover. I made a promise to myself that I will allow my body to relax. My body is free to feel everything she cares to feel and express and then some. I promised myself I would welcome it all. I could feel an opening in my heart. I could feel my entire body relax. I cried my eyes out on the floor. This was the message I'd been waiting for all these years and years.

When I first begin to explore my sexuality, I didn't yet know enough about how my body worked, and therefore, how my heart worked. My first beloved, Jeffrey, didn't mean to shame me. We thought there was something wrong. Later, I discovered something completely different. Without education, shame can taint our sexual experiences.

Why do we still whisper about female ejaculation? Why are we not teaching our daughters and our sons about this phenomenon? It is still shrouded in secrecy and probably in grief, too. How can something so perfectly mysterious be anything but divine in nature? Lovers who have no information beyond the most basic of basics, who are just following their intuition and instinct end up hurting each other, wounding each other so profoundly. We need more tenderness. We need more self-love.

My first lover thought he had a bed-wetter on his hands, but really, he had a Goddess-in-Training. He was blessed. I was blessed. I'm glad to know it now.

Sacred sex is not for the weak at heart. Sex is for the brave souls who are willing to be vulnerable and get their egos out of the game. Sex is for tender adventurers. Sex is for all of us, in all of our bodies and all of the amazing things they know how to do.

In Tantra, Amrita is considered to be a blessing for the woman who experiences it and for her partner. It's not urine. It's something completely different. It may be even holy. It's part of my orgasm; it's part of my communion with my lover and with the Divine. I'm finally able to accept that my body does this in those rare moments of supreme joy and when I am in love, held by the Divine, and floating in bliss.

About the Author
Jennifer Lakshmi Dove Robinson

www.jenniferlakshmidoverobinson.com

What did you want to be when you were eight years old?

When I was eight years old I was in training to be a mermaid. My family lived in Florida, and it was a magical time for me. I was growing my hair down to my waist. I had seen mermaids many times at Weeki Wachee, and I practiced in my neighbor's pool every chance I got.

If you could give one piece of advice to your younger self about your orgasm, what would it be?

Be not afraid. What the body does is sacred. Don't let anyone talk you out of your own pleasure. Sometimes the things that have the most power take the longest to understand. Have patience, sweetheart. You will find your way.

SIXTEEN

"You've got the words to change a nation
But you're biting your tongue
You've spent a lifetime stuck in silence
Afraid you'll say something wrong
If no one ever hears it, how we gonna learn your song?"

—lyrics from *Read All About It Pt III*,
Emeli Sandé

THE DEATH OF HYMEN
by SL Sourwine

Sometimes the story of an orgasm has to begin with the emancipation of your female body for service to yourself and not to a culture that would make it, including its potential for pleasure, serve something else. Sometimes pleasure itself can remind you that you can be free. The story of my orgasm and me is a story of knots.

I vividly remember one night when I was a small child – my parents brought home a huge pile of discarded costume jewelry from the department store where my mom worked. It was all to be thrown out, because somehow it had ended up in a mound of knots, kinks, and snarls. The huge, glittery pile of potential wonders and unknown worth was dumped on our smooth freezer top. We could glimpse a pendant here, a medallion there, but we couldn't immediately extricate them from the maze. The story of my orgasm has been like teasing those beautiful things free.

Reclaiming dominion over my own body from the family history, institutions and dictatorships of thought that contorted my understanding of it has been very important to me. Like navigating the labyrinth of chains and bracelets in that jumble, it can be slow work. So much time and effort to untangle the ideas implanted in me: isolating, sourcing, cataloguing, and estimating. And yet often, almost magically, one small tug will release another extraordinary treasure.

My journey has been both satisfyingly difficult and frighteningly pleasurable. Satisfying, because I have been bred to revel in the struggle of building on what I have been given. Hard work pays. To do so on your own behalf is a privilege, and it's rewarding. The satisfaction powers the determination to sit and begin to unravel the first strand of the hoard. My journey has been frightening, because pleasure can be a very formidable force. The entire flow of pleasure sits in opposition to struggle. Your pleasure is the thing they have been warning you about, protecting you from, and shaming you for. Claiming your pleasure and its impact feels dangerous. Vulnerable. Unruly. Visible.

My pleasure can make me feel like a wobbly-legged, shiny, gloriously surrendered heap of happy mush – oh, the feeling of allowing myself to be unraveled, to feel pleasure's alchemical state! When I accede to my pleasure, whether it's an orgasm or the intake of beauty that moves me, the world reorganizes around me. Some of the tangled pieces begin to move of their own accord, but I can't control which ones. I have to trust it. In the early days of my journey, there was no way I was going to allow pleasure's extreme vulnerability. I could not even conceive of a space safe enough to feel that exposed. However, an external location was not what was required. I needed to fight for my body.

One of those surprise extrications occurred for me recently. I recognized exactly when the quest for my body had started. It began at the beginning of my personal sexual journey. Not at the sexual gratification taken at my expense from my body by my father when I was a child. Nor did it start the first time I had sex, although the fun of finally "doing it" with a two-stepping cowboy from a town called Big Beaver will always give me a goofy smile. None of those were the beginning for me.

My quest to free myself began the night I murdered Hymen.

I wasn't the most informed of young girls. I read my sister's copy of *Are You There, God? It's Me, Margaret*, dwelled on the teenage sex scenes in Forever, and listened mesmerized to discussions of losing your virginity: who you gave it to, what you saved it for. I was curious, despite myself. My own books were all about horses and dogs and wilderness adventure, but the world around me was changing. Sex started to be everywhere. I had thought that when we escaped my father, I was done having to worry about sex. But there it was, all around me and even inside me. I was angry about the disruption of puberty, uniformed, and very aware of the need for the emancipation of my female flesh from an unnamed something. Even before I had the words, before I knew all the stories, I was pissed off by the imperialism virginity enacted on my female body.

I'm trying to remember all the details from the night I killed Hymen. Why was it so necessary to banish this intruder? How did my 12 year-old self understand that? Was it rage that some unknown male god of marriage roosted between my legs? That my body was simply the vessel, bearing his gift to the man I was to surrender it to, like a pretty box in which his prize was presented to him? Or was I like an oyster after the pearl is taken, consumed or discarded? Was it curiosity as my older friends described their first sexual encounters and the playful insertion of body parts and other experiments? Was it anger at the saccharine stories of teenage love that Hymen preciously bestowed on the worthy sweetheart (who for me was nowhere in sight)?

All this fuss over Hymen. Why was I not allowed to choose what gods I served? I was really more into Artemis – I wanted only time amongst my creatures and books, my body free for exploring and searching, roaming and finding. There was no space for a bloody possession such as Hymen inside my chaste teen loves. I longed for closeness with another, and yet distance from what I knew about the body's betrayal and pain. But Hymen was everywhere. Interrupting. At school, in my home, in my sister's books… this Hymen pressured me to decide whose gift he was and how it would be given.

I would not have it. I would not be added to his lists, counted and verified. It was mine. My body was mine. That was something I knew very clearly, and yet the world, the stories, my father, and the experiences of others kept trying to insist differently. There was no space for this Hymen fellow between my legs. I'm afraid my emancipation was ripe, and I was quite insistent on it.

Of course, I had no idea of altars beyond the one at the front of our small Catholic church. Catholic altars were places for men and boys; I was only to approach with my head bowed. But alone in my room, I lay back on the furry, wild horses covered bedspread. Porcelain idols of happy dogs and mythical horses lined up, encircling me to bear witness – what a little priestess I was! I can sense the weight of the pale, smooth-handled hairbrush in my hand still. I can feel the plastic, warm from my touch, and watch the lacy sleeve of my sweet, thin, cotton nightgown sliding down my arm as I held up the brush. I spread my own legs and began pushing it into me. There were no guides, no anointing, no sharing of knowledge to ease my way. I was alone. I trusted only myself to touch me.

I took my virginity for myself.

Hymen's death would be no one's gift or sacrament.

There was no pleasure.

There was no loss.

It was one of the least desperate acts of my life. Actually, I'm surprised more girls don't do it. It would certainly put an end to auctioning it, verifying it, and prophets' promises to bestow it upon warriors in paradise. I love her, me, for being so fierce in that moment. I haven't always been so fearless on the quest, and I've even abandoned myself a few times along the way.

The discovery of the power of my pleasure is tied for me to the ongoing reclamation of my body. It is a journey, sometimes with a partner, sometimes surrounded by my sister-women on the same journey, and sometimes alone like I was that night. My ability to allow and experience the gift of my orgasm, and the scope of the pleasure I am capable of receiving, is linked to how safe I feel inside my own body. To learn to feel safe, welcome, and yes, even glorious in my own body is my epic.

About the Author
SL Sourwine

What did you want to be when you were eight years old?

A veterinarian.

If you could give one piece of advice to your younger self about your orgasm, what would it be?

It's ok for you to feel that much in your body. Your body is your ally, not your enemy.

SEVENTEEN

"Be free and shine like always."

—Santiago

REFLECTIONS OF SUNSHINE
by Jaylin Madison

I declined an invitation to have dinner with co-workers, and I walked down to the starlit beach of a remote island is Southern Thailand. I needed to clear my head if I was going to stay here for seven more days. This wasn't the first time I had been here. In fact, I was the one who suggested we shoot an episode of our travel show here, but now I questioned my own judgment about returning. When I reached the shoreline, I breathed in the warm night air, thick with condensation and memories. Far from the island's few huts and restaurants, I crumpled to my knees, grasped a handful of soft, white sand and closed my eyes. Instantly I was 27 years old again, sitting at the exact spot on the beach where I'd been seven years earlier. The soft, warm breeze brushed against my skin like his gentle fingers once did. The humid salt-water air hung on my lips like his breath. I could still hear his laugh echoing off of the limestone cliffs that hugged the shoreline.

I was younger then, but I knew Great Love when I found it. I had quit my job in Corporate America and set out to explore Southeast Asia on my own. I met Johan on a night bus from Bangkok, and I was drawn to him immediately. He had piercing blue eyes, curly light brown hair and a smile that could light up the darkest of nights, with a perfect little gap between his teeth. It was the most beautiful smile I had ever seen. Within three days of traveling together, I fell in love with the free-spirited Norwegian, and we decided not to be apart from then on. He was charmingly witty, refreshingly honest and genuinely kind. He introduced me to new ways of thinking, kept his cool when we lost our luggage and made passionate love to me under the stars. We traveled throughout the country together for a month, making our way from the hill tribe villages in the North to the tropical beaches in the South. Once there, Johan embraced my idea to go off the beaten track and hire a boat to take us to a remote island not listed in any guidebooks. He was always up for an adventure, and that's how we found ourselves here.

The photo I had taken of this spot on the beach remained as my desktop screensaver long after I had broken Johan's heart. Long after I had not been brave enough to see our love through. Long after I had chosen an easier route, dating someone who lived down the street instead of across the world. Johan begged me to reconsider, but I didn't have the patience and faith that he had, and I let my Great Love slip through my fingers. Right before I returned to film here, I'd heard that he was engaged to someone else.

I crawled to a seated position and looked out over the ocean. Stars shone directly above me, but out over the water there was a dark storm brewing. I could see the black clouds covering the night sky where the water dropped off the edge of the earth. I sighed heavily and spoke to the sky, as I sometimes do on dark nights of the soul.

"I know that this bizarre set of circumstances that brought me back here must be for a reason, but I can barely breathe here. I loved him so much, and I held myself back. You've asked me to let go of so many things lately. The job I've had for years, the home I loved, most of my belongings. And here I sit in the same spot where I was with Johan, and I see that I haven't even begun to let go of anything."

I admitted to the heavens all the heaviness in my heart, the guilt I'd been carrying, and the deep remorse I felt then, single and 34. And, as if in response to my streaming tears, lightning began to dance in the distance. I spilled my heart out to the sky for over an hour and the clouds replied with pulses of illuminated energy over the ocean.

When my tears had run empty, I said out loud, "Right here, in this personally sacred spot, I forgive myself. Great Love is my destiny, and my timing is perfect."

And just then, the lightning stopped, and the sky became completely still. I held my breath. Had the night communicated with me so poetically just to leave me alone at such a pivotal moment of surrender? Then, a small lightning bug caught my eye as it flew toward my face and danced around my head. I had never seen a lightning bug on this beach before (and I never saw one again). Goosebumps ran up my spine as the lightning fluttered quietly and intimately beside me. My heart breathed a sigh of release.

I thanked the sky for my profound experience and followed the lights up to the beach bar where my co-workers were having cocktails. Refreshed and renewed, I pulled up a chair in the sand to join them. I smiled at their conversation but didn't speak much. I knew that what I had just experienced was nothing short of miraculous, but I told myself that no one else would understand, so I'd keep the story to myself.

That's when I saw him.

He had sun-kissed brown skin, black hair and strong muscles toned from years of rock climbing. His eyes caught mine, and I could see the light of his presence shining through them. He took my breath away when he smiled in my direction and walked towards the empty chair next to mine.

"It's okay for me to sit here, with you?" he asked with a thick Spanish accent.

"I think this seat has your name on it," I replied.

"I'm Santiago, nice to meet you," the words rolled off of his tongue.

Santiago was from Spain, and had left his job two years ago to follow his dream of traveling the world. He had one more year to go before he returned to his home. He told me how deeply the experience of travel was affecting him. How he was feeling like the most blessed man on the planet. How this experience was opening his eyes and awakening his soul. How he was beginning to see love everywhere.

"And you can, too, if you choose to see it," he smiled.

I told him about my experience on the beach, and he listened intently. I thought of how ironic it was that I had just told myself that I would never speak of this story, and here I was, sharing it fifteen minutes later with a stranger.

We had a few drinks at the bar and lingered long past the time when my crew had moved on to another bar. Everything else seemed to stop when Santiago's dark eyes were focused solely on me.

"Should we go to meet our friends?" he asked finally.

"Let's go," I replied.

We walked together as the beach trail turned inland and became a narrow jungle path. We made our way through the dense green leaves, over the root systems breaking through the path, and he held my hand so I wouldn't lose my footing. We laughed like old friends, and it felt glorious to be enjoying the moment instead of drowning in memories.

We reached the second outdoor bar in time to see the fire dancers taking turns balancing on a thin slack line suspended in the air. Music pulsed in the background, and crickets accompanied the song. It seemed like a lifetime ago that I felt unhappy about being on this island. When the show was over, we took turns trying our skills at balancing on the slack line. Santiago went first and crossed the suspended wire with ease and grace. Everything he did was smooth and sexy – the way he spoke. The way he walked. The way he balanced on a slack line.

"Your turn, love," he said.

I made several attempts and never got farther than two steps until Santiago went to the opposite side of the line. His eyes locked on mine. "Come to me. Now. Just do it."

I took a deep breath and took two steps. Then three. Then four, then five. Six. Seven! I crossed the line and fell into Santiago's arms. He wrapped them tightly around me and kissed my lips. I felt energy shooting across my stomach like the lightning bolts from the sky.

"I… I could," he stuttered when our eyes opened, "I could love you." His big, brown eyes were surprised at his own words.

"That's very brave of you to say. Thank you," I replied.

"Come. Walk back to the beach with me."

We sat on the sand together in the same spot where I had been just hours earlier. There was no trace of the dark clouds anymore, just a sky full of diamond stars. Santiago snuggled close to me. He reached over and touched the skin on my ankles. His fingers moved slowly up my legs.

"Lie back," he said.

I lay down, my back supported by the white sand. He slowly moved to face me and lovingly drew patterns on the skin of my legs, exposed by my short shorts. I sighed at the gentle touch of his fingers and of the warm breeze that accompanied them. He spread my legs open and knelt between them. He unzipped his zipper and reached into his shorts to reveal his dark, erect penis. I lifted myself onto my elbows.

"Santiago. I think you're incredible, and we've had the best night, but I'd like to take things a little bit more slowly," I said

"As you wish," he replied, "but, it's okay if I touch your leg… here?"

"Yes."

"And… here?" he said with a smile, zipping his pants back up.

"Yes."

"And how about… here?" He moved his hands further up my thigh.

"Anywhere my skin is exposed at this moment is okay," I said.

"Ahh, okay." He kissed my legs, and my arms, and bits of my exposed navel, and I relaxed into the sand.

For the next several days, my co-workers and I wandered around the island, diving and filming. Swimming and filming. Rock climbing and filming. And every once in a while, I would look across the beach to find Santiago returning from a rock climb. He would stop to watch us work until he caught my eyes, smiled, and continued on his way. We met up several times for a drink, or for a meal, or to perfect our slack lining skills.

Santiago had been on the island for over a month already, and he knew nearly everyone there by name. I was struck by how people gravitated towards him. The women on the island were drawn to him, blushing and giggling. The men would stop to give him a long bear hug. Even the young boy at the late-night pancake stand lit up when Santiago came to place his nightly order for a banana pancake with Nutella.

"Do people often tell you that you're like the sunshine?" I asked with a mouth full of pancake one night.

"How do you mean?" he said.

"I see light shining from your eyes, and I watch how men, women, children, locals, foreigners, everyone…they all love to bask in this light. They circle around you like planets around the sun. Do people tell you that you're like the sunshine?"

He leaned in towards me. "Here is a secret, my Queen," he whispered. "I give people my full attention, and maybe they feel that. So, the answer to your question is no. Not many say this to me. Because not many can see as you do. Only those who possess that same light can see it in others." Then he held my face and kissed me. "Stay with me tonight, in my hut. No sex, this is fine. But sleep next to me this night. Let me dream about you while I dream next to you."

I agreed.

Santiago's little hut was cozy and sweet, built on stilts, with walls constructed from palm trees. We crawled under the mosquito net and curled up together. He shared some of his favorite songs from his iPod, his favorite passages from the books he'd been reading on the road, some of his favorite treasures given to him along his journey – a seashell from someone special, a t-shirt from a friend, a water bottle from someone who had little to give.

I tried to sleep that night, but I lay awake long after he had drifted off. An hour, then two, then three crept by. I had a shoot early in the morning and I was sharing a cabin with a co-worker. What would they think when I wasn't there? What if I couldn't sleep? What if falling for Santiago would break my heart? My mind raced and I could feel myself begin to panic.

"I'm so sorry." I woke him. "I have to go."

"What, love? No, please stay. Let me hold you," he replied in a fog.

"I must go." I lifted the mosquito net and crawled out of his bed.

He sat up. "What is happening? Have I upset you?"

"Not at all," I said. "It's not you, I'm not used to sleeping next to someone, and I've got to sleep."

"I am sad to see you leaving my bed," he said, and he rolled over.

The next morning, I worked with my friends, and I did not see Santiago. I went to the lunch spot he frequented, and he wasn't there. We filmed in the afternoon, and Santiago didn't walk by. I didn't see him until the evening.

I approached him as he ate with a large group of Spanish-speaking friends, "Hola, Santiago."

"Hola, darling," he smiled. "Such a strange thing for you to leave me in the night."

I pulled up a chair next to him. "I know. I…" I whispered so his friends wouldn't hear. "I couldn't sleep."

He held my face close to his. "Your mind is very busy most of the time."

His brown sunshine eyes made me smile. "Yes, it can be."

"You are welcome to try again tonight. I would love to hold you for as long into the night as you wish."

That night, I slept next to Santiago all night. I was asleep long before he was, and every time I awoke, I was aware that his body was wrapped around me tightly.

The following day, I announced to my friends that I would not be joining them on the shoot. I wasn't needed, and I wanted to spend the day with Santiago. He and I ate a fresh fruit breakfast and dashed into the sea for a long swim in the warm, salty water. He told me stories that embarrassed him, stories that broke his heart, stories that made us both laugh until our sides hurt. We splashed and played. It was a beautiful, perfect afternoon.

That evening, we sat on the porch of his little hut and I doctored some of his cuts and bruises from weeks of climbing. The next day I would be taking a boat back to Bangkok, and the following day I'd be flying back to California.

"Or…." he said, "You could change your ticket. Stay here, with me. Unpack your things and be my guest in my hut. I would love to see your femininity spill all over this space."

My mind raced again. What would my co-workers think? What would the Executive Producer of the show say? I felt guilty for just taking the day off.

He walked into the hut, and returned quickly. "Here," he said, revealing a small coin in his hand "If it is heads you will go tomorrow. Tails you will stay for more days."

"Oh, it's that easy?" I laughed.

He threw the coin into the air, and caught it, covering the outcome with his other hand. "Now," he said. "Which do you want it to be? Heads, go? Or tails, stay?"

I closed my eyes and felt deeply into the question. "Tails. I want to stay with you," I said. "Which is it?"

"Ahh…the outcome from the coin doesn't matter. What matters is that now you know how you feel." He smiled and tossed the coin back into the doorway.

I laughed, "I will think about it. But for now, I should have dinner with my co-workers. I haven't seen them all day."

"As you wish," he replied.

I ate with my small crew, and we made our game plan for the boat hire and the transportation back to Bangkok early the next morning. They all retired to their rooms early to finish packing. I said I had something to check online, and I went to the Internet cafe. A half hour later, I had changed my ticket. I would stay on the island for three more days.

I waved to my friends as their small boat pulled off of the beach at 8:00 the following morning, and I practically ran to Santiago's door when they were out of sight. I was elated to have given myself three more days on this beach with him. Funny how at one point, seven days here seemed like a punishment. Now, it wasn't enough time.

I moved into Santiago's hut, and we had another beautiful day together. That night after dinner, we got caught in a thunderous rainstorm. The small dirt paths became thick with rich, dark mud, and we were soaked within minutes. We danced in the warm rain until it became a torrential downpour, and we retreated to the hut early, laughing at each other's drenched-to-the-bone exteriors as we kicked off our muddy flip-flops. The rain pounded against the tin roof, and thunder rocked the hut. Lightning illuminated Santiago's face, and then the darkness hid him from my view again.

"Sunshine," I said over the rain's patter. I had been calling him that for days now.

"Yes, darling," he answered.

"Take my shirt off for me?"

"Yes." He made his way over to me and gently removed my rain soaked t-shirt.

"And my skirt — it's so wet," I said.

He moved his hands down to my waist and pulled my skirt to my ankles. I stepped out of it.

"My panties. They're wet, too," I smiled.

"Yes," he agreed as he moved his hand inside of my panties and felt just how wet I was truly becoming. He removed them slowly.

He stood to look at me. "And this," I said, as I removed my bra and threw it to the floor.

The lightning flashed and lit my naked body standing before him. He removed his clothes and grabbed my hips as he kissed my lips. I loved the feel of his tongue inside my mouth, his hands exploring the skin on my backside, his hard cock pushing against my leg. Thunder shook the hut and he pulled me into him more tightly. I ached for him to be inside me.

He moved towards the bed and crawled under the mosquito net. I grabbed a condom from my bag and joined him there.

He lay on his back, and I straddled his dark body, running my hands over the soft skin of his chest before holding his perfect brown penis in my mouth. He groaned. I teased him with my tongue and moaned at the taste of him as he entered my mouth over and over.

When he pulled himself out, he gently rolled me onto my back. He looked deeply into my eyes. He spoke to me in Spanish, lovingly and sweetly as he touched my face. I couldn't understand his words, but I didn't need to.

He tickled my thighs with his fingers and kissed them gently with his mouth before making his way to my outer lips. He kissed me gently there and sucked on my skin before making his way to my clitoris. I groaned in pleasure and was lost in the waves of ecstasy and intensity. I came back to consciousness before I reached orgasm, and I rolled Santiago over onto his back. My pussy pulsed with desire, and I was wetter than the rain-soaked jungle outside.

I put the condom on his enlarged penis, and I straddled him. He slid into me slowly and we both moaned.

"Yes. Yesssss," he yelled over the rain. It pounded against the tin roof harder now, and I could barely hear his words. The lightening flashed again, and the thunder followed. The storm was right on top of us. I directed his thumb to the tip of my clitoris. I wanted to feel him deeply inside of me and also to feel the nerve endings of my clitoris sending signals of pleasure to my entire being. We melted together in rapture and passion. With each thrust of his cock, I gasped. I grew short of breath, and the whole room began to spin. I moaned loudly. The heavy rain gave us both the freedom to be loud with passion. It turned me on intensely, and my pussy contracted to pull him even more deeply inside.

He turned me over onto my belly and entered me from behind. He pushed his soft skin against my backside and pressed his cheek against my face. His lips were near my ear, and he spoke to me again in Spanish. I could feel his breath near my face as he thrust into me, slowly this time. My body arched in elation, and I pushed my backside harder into his pelvis. He moved slowly now, and my body craved more.

I turned over, and he pushed himself back inside me, this time looking into my eyes. He tried to move his mouth to speak, but what spilled out from his lips was a whimper. He kept his eyes locked on me as we rocked back and forth in interconnection. I couldn't tell where his body ended and mine began

We rolled over together one last time, our bodies not coming apart. I rode him in rhythm, gasping for air as the rain pummeled the tin roof in a deafening sound of release from the sky. He moved more quickly inside of me now, and I felt myself building and building. Santiago howled in ecstatic liberation as he released into the latex barrier. I could feel the condom fill inside of me.

I felt seen, adored, desired, and then, vulnerable. I knew that he had almost taken me over an edge that I had never quite been over. I had come to orgasm before, but as connected and open as I felt at that moment, I stopped myself. And then, when I couldn't stop myself, I began to cry. I cried because I needed to release. I cried because I wanted to go over the edge. I cried for all the times I'd held myself back because of fear, including this time. I cried because I already missed Santiago.

He stroked my hair with his fingers and held me close.

"Do you feel this?" he asked, putting his hands over my heart.

I inhaled, "I feel you very deeply there."

"I am planting a seed here," he whispered. "I am planting a seed of love in your heart, and every day this seed will grow. The next time I see you, it will be a strong and beautiful tree. And you will not be so afraid."

Three days later, I was on a small boat, pulling away from the sandy shoreline that I had come to know so well. Santiago stood on the beach with his hands in his pockets. His eyes were darker and larger than I had seen them before. I hadn't felt a pull to another person like that in a long, long time. Maybe not since the last time I said goodbye to someone I loved on the same beach. I waved to him, and he nodded slowly, but didn't remove his hands from his pockets. The space between us increased rapidly, and I watched him stand alone on the sand until he was a small dot in the distance. That's when the island came into full view.

"Thank you," I whispered.

And then, when I was ready, I turned away from the island that had called me back.

At home I found myself thinking about Santiago often, and I pulled an Oracle Card for some insight. The card I pulled was the Merlin, and the description read, "The Merlin is the masculine keeper of magic, capable of turning iron into gold. He will lend you his wisdom on this leg of your journey until you can claim it as your own. But remember, all signs and omens sent from the Merlin are but reflections of that which is already in you."

Last I heard, Santiago was back in Spain and had met the love of his life. And as for me, I am beginning to see love everywhere. Great Love is my destiny, and my timing is perfect. I have a tree of love in my heart and sunshine in my eyes.

About the Author
Jaylin Madison

What did you want to be when you were eight years old?

When I was eight years old, I wanted to be a teacher. That was the year I made my first movie, though, with my neighbors, friends and little brother. I have been making shows, movies and videos ever since.

If you could give one piece of advice to your younger self about your orgasm, what would it be?

Sex is a beautiful, powerful, sacred expression, not the feared path to transgression that you were told. With reverence and connection, orgasm is capable of deepening your sense of self, your connection to another person and your experience of God.

If your orgasm had a voice, what would your orgasm say to you about the piece you wrote for this book?

Orgasm is not a goal to attain or a peak to reach, but a continual process of evolution and a courageous expansion into LOVE.

EIGHTEEN

Everyone
Is God speaking.
Why not be polite and
Listen to
Him?

—Hafiz

MAKING NOISE
by Betsy Blankenbaker

For many years, I heard the phrase "body, mind, spirit" to describe what makes up "me", but I never got the message to value my body in the same way I honored my mind through study and my spirit through prayer. I chose to disconnect from my body after a pattern of sexual assault that began when I was young and continued into my forties. I was not friends with my vagina, and until I starting researching my orgasm at age forty-five, I was clueless about my body's potential to feel good.

One of the most challenging things for me during my orgasm research was speaking up for myself. For years I had stayed quiet, whether it was about something that didn't feel good in bed or about someone who hurt me. I ignored the power and truth in my voice as much as I ignored the desires of my vagina. We were both lonely.

I always stayed quiet when my boyfriends made love to me. I never asked for what I wanted. I willingly offered my body, even when what they were doing to me didn't feel good. I was a master at disconnecting from my body to protect myself from feeling any sensations that could elicit the shame and pain from the original abuse.

When I started my orgasm research and forced myself to be present with my feelings and the sensations in my body, I finally had to give a voice to my orgasm. She liked to speak up – not too loud, but she wanted to be respected, and I realized that by staying quiet all those years, I was dishonoring my body and my voice. I was not respecting my essence. I was not listening.

In my research, I found by inhaling deep into my pelvis and humming or moaning on the exhale, I could feel more of my orgasmic sensations. Using my voice allowed my orgasm to go from being a short, quick release, like men experience, to waves of orgasmic climaxes. The full deep circular breaths send fresh oxygen into my genitals, and the sounds vibrate from my throat down my spine, through the walls of my vagina and out through my clitoris. Each cycle of breath and sound extend my orgasm longer and take my body higher into an ecstatic state expanding my orgasm from seconds to minutes to hours. It's my choice. I just have to use my voice.

Tantra teacher Charles Muir said, "In America, most women make more sound eating their dessert than they do in orgasm." We definitely need to get more comfortable using our voices! Making sounds and giving verbal cues improves the quality and length of our orgasm. It's also a way of letting our partners know we approve of what they are during. If you don't have a partner, allow your orgasm to speak during self-pleasuring. By not making noise we are disowning our voices and our bodies and missing out on feeling all of our orgasm. The consequences of staying quiet can go way beyond having a satisfying orgasm.

In my book, *Autobiography of an Orgasm*, I wrote candidly about my experience of being sexually assaulted many times and not speaking up because of the shame and judgment I knew I might face. It was something "we just don't talk about" and I thought I was the only one who had experienced it. I finally told my story because I wanted to give a voice to the six year old that was too confused and afraid to speak up. I also wanted to honor the 40 year old woman in me that was raped during a party and still stayed quiet. I'm not too sure the man, who was intoxicated, thinks what he did was wrong because I never said anything. It was another secret that I kept to myself until a few years later, when another friend mentioned that she felt she had been raped by him. As sad as I was for her experience of assault by the same man, it was a relief that I wasn't alone. And then I wondered, what if I spoke up sooner? What if I said something to him so he knew his behavior was not acceptable. Maybe it would have saved my friend. Maybe it would have saved others.

One of the letters I received from a woman in her thirties who read *Autobiography of an Orgasm* described her disconnection from her body after rape and assault in college: "I can't even begin to express how much I was affected by your book. It brought up so much for me. I have never seen myself as worthy of enjoying life in general, and being sexually satisfied was definitely not even a blip on my radar. My mother was hateful and angry all the time from being raped in her youth, and so I grew up always hearing about how horrible men were. Then I went off to college where I was held in a frat boy's room against my will, where numerous guys molested me followed by laughter and mocking. The icing on the cake was that they used razors to cut me so I would be ugly to everyone else. They said they would be the only people that would want to see me naked. I am covered in scars, and for a long time I believed them, and if I am being honest, I guess I still do. I don't talk about this story very much (pretty much never), so it is surprising me that I am telling it to you now."

It's estimated that 90% of acquaintance rapes don't speak up, and many of these happen in high school or the first years of college where alcohol is a factor in 90% of the cases. We are seeing more and more stories of girls committing suicide after being assaulted by someone they know or dying as a result of a night of extreme partying. In too many of these cases there are other people around taking photos or videos or helping dispose of the body, but rarely is someone speaking up and saying "Stop" or "Let me get you home safely and stay with you until you are better."

There was another incident of assault that I didn't write about in my book because he was a popular Lama with many followers. I admired the message he brings to the western world, but I stopped admiring the messenger when this Lama groped me and pushed his tongue into my mouth. Up until that moment, I had never touched this man; I had only treated him with reverence, bowing when I saw him out of respect for his position. At the time, I was making a film about him (this was 2002 - 2004). When the uninvited groping happened, I was meeting him in his room to take him to where I would be interviewing him a few minutes later. After I pushed him away, I didn't say a word except, "We are ready for the interview." And then I walked out and spent the next thirty minutes interviewing him on camera. I didn't mention the incident in his room a few minutes earlier.

I was 39, and what I can say is my body and mind went into "shock" mode. I just focused on what I was supposed to do – interview this man for a documentary. Later I mentioned what had happened to my boyfriend at the time, and to my cameraman, and to another friend who was a photographer on the project. I even continued to work on the film a little longer until I heard from another woman that she felt she had also been taken advantage of by this Lama. I finally stopped making the film, because every time I saw this man's face on screen, I felt violated. Part of me wondered if maybe I just didn't understand his culture; maybe he didn't mean to force himself on me. Later I found out it had happened to other women, too.

Recently, I watched a CNN story on Bikram Choudhury (the founder of the Bikram yoga movement). He was responding to allegations of rape by several of his former students. I know two of those students and I believe they were raped by Bikram. His response to the charges was that he doesn't need to sexually assault anyone because so many women love him; he wouldn't have to force himself on anyone. Through his tears he added, "Shame on western culture" for doing this to him. That statement sent a surge of rage through my body.

The poet Maya Angelou wrote, "I come as one, I stand as 10,000." We as women and the men who love us can't afford to not speak up anymore. There is power in our voice. We need to remember our bodies as sacred no matter what has happened to us. And we need to remember to choose love over fear when making decisions on whether to reveal ourselves. I am done being shamed or being quiet and I know I am not standing alone. The only way to honor my body is to speak up and make noise, whether it's to stop the ongoing assault of girls and women or to bring my orgasm to climax.

About the Author
Betsy Blankenbaker

www.betsyblankenbaker.com

Betsy can be contacted at aoaothebook@gmail.com
or you can 'Follow' her on Facebook: Betsy Blankenbaker

What is your orgasm saying to you lately?

With the release of my book *Autobiography of an Orgasm*, I finally chose to let my soul breathe. My friend and shamanic astrologer Sao describes how our soul breathes: "Your body breathes through inhale and exhale. Your soul breathes through experience and express. Experience and express."

One of the first things I notice when I'm not fully expressing myself is my breath is shallow. I may become edgy and unfocused. Sometimes, I even get a sore throat. These are some of the signs that remind me I'm holding onto things — keeping things inside. Maybe I'm not speaking up because I'm worried about what others will think so I choose to betray myself instead of others.

And then a song or a sunrise or a soulful conversation will bring me back to listening to my body and I remember what I need to say, and I say it out loud or I dance it through my body. It doesn't matter if anyone is watching or listening. What matters is that I let my soul breathe. I express myself.

After releasing *Autobiography of an Orgasm*, I started receiving letters and messages from women and a few men who read the book and were affected by my choice to tell such a vulnerable story.

"Thank you for speaking up."

"This is a courageous book."

"You've shown me how to stop judging myself and appreciate myself instead."

"I was meant to read your book. I see myself in your story and now I see that I can heal too."

"Your book made me excited about exploring sex again instead of being ashamed."

"You are changing the world and how we think about sex."

What is the story of your orgasm? Do you have a story you would like to be considered for the next edition of *Autobiographies of Our Orgasms?* This isn't *50 Shades of Grey*. It's women and men telling true stories from their sensual paths. Ideally, you will choose to write and publish under your name, but it you aren't ready to speak up with your name attached, you can choose to write under a pseudonym.

To be considered for the book, please submit your story of up to 4,000 words to: aoaothebook@gmail.com.

Remember your soul needs to breathe.

Experience. Express. Experience. Express

ACKNOWLEDGEMENTS

Thank you to my children Sam, Lucy, Willie and Charlie for being so understanding and supportive when I chose to write about orgasm.

Thank you to Paul Yinger for the beautiful cover designs for this book and for *Autobiography of an Orgasm*. Thank you for making my Os look so good!

Thank you to Tara for dancing with me in both the light and the shadow.

Thank you to my friend, novelist and writing teacher Dan Wakefield, for standing for my orgasm, my books and my films.

Thank you to the Smith sisters, Amy & Lauren, for including me as a sister.

Thank you to favorite friends and boutiques for carrying *Autobiography of an Orgasm*: Jen at *Flea Market Chic* (Indiana); Vicki at *The Playful Soul* (Indianapolis); Yaf at *YafSparkle* (New York City); and, Karen at *En Avance* (Miami).

Thank you to my friend Rochelle Schieck for creating Qoya (loveqoya.com) so I could remember my body and life as sacred.

Thank you to my friend Sao for reminding me that writing is how my soul breathes.

Thank you to my fantastic copy editor (and sometimes cheerleader), Amanda Coffin.

Thank you to all the writers featured in this book for writing about events in their lives, especially the moments that felt too private to tell but that you wrote down anyway. Through your stories, we remember that our lives matter and that love is always present, even in the times when we felt the most alone, abandoned or betrayed. Your stories show us how you danced the path back to yourselves and remind us that we can find our way home, too.

Made in the USA
Middletown, DE
20 May 2015